FINAL
SCORE!

DAN FARR

FINAL SCORE!
IN THE PAINT

TATE PUBLISHING
AND ENTERPRISES, LLC

Published by Tate Publishing & Enterprises, LLC
127 E. Trade Center Terrace | Mustang, Oklahoma 73064 USA
1.888.361.9473 | www.tatepublishing.com

Tate Publishing is committed to excellence in the publishing industry. The company reflects the philosophy established by the founders, based on Psalm 68:11,
"The Lord gave the word and great was the company of those who published it."

Book design copyright © 2014 by Tate Publishing, LLC. All rights reserved.
Cover design by Allen Jomoc
Interior design by Jake Muelle

Published in the United States of America

ISBN: 978-1-63306-196-5
Sports & Recreation / Basketball
14.07.23

This is for my best friend and wonderful wife, Becca, and to our daughters, Allison and Jillian. This book is in memory of my father, Lester E. Farr Sr., my mother, Allene Farr, and my father-in-law, Damon Ray.

CONTENTS

INTRODUCTION

Do you know a young person (or an adult) who is crazy about sports but you can't seem to get through to them about their need for Christ? I was once that person, and God used sports to get me, at the age of forty-eight, to see what Christ had done on the cross for me. This book is designed to help you break through the barrier.

Through this collection of devotions and short stories, I have attempted to combine my knowledge of sports, my growing knowledge of the Bible, and my everyday experiences to connect the reader to the gospel in a fresh, new way. Hopefully one of these stories will reach a young man or young woman for Christ who otherwise might have never known him. Everyone needs to understand that it is very cool to know Jesus and for him to know us.

Jesus taught the people two thousand years ago using ordinary stories about farming, water, marriage, and everyday life called parables. If Jesus wrote parables today, undoubtedly, he would toss in a few sports stories since so many people today are passionate about sports. The Apostle Paul shared in 1 Corinthians 9:22, "Whatever a person is like, I try to find common ground with him, so that he will let me tell him about Christ, and let Christ save him" (TLB). My hope and prayer is to share these sports-related parables in a way that the lightbulb will come on for you to enable you to look at the cross as you never have before and allow God to change you and disciple you. To God be all the glory that might result from this book.

.

TESTIMONY

I am honored and privileged to share my testimony with you. On a Sunday morning in the late 1960s in a small Methodist church in middle Georgia, I could have received Christ. I was drawn to Jesus Christ by the Holy Spirit during a message by a lay speaker, but I was afraid of what people would say if I went to the altar. I escaped into the warm sunshine and convinced myself that I would have enough nerve to accept Christ the following Sunday. But I went back into the wilderness for thirty-five years. I did not attend church when I moved to Atlanta, but I met my future wife, Becca, through the sports ministry at Peachtree Presbyterian Church. We married the following year and were later blessed with two beautiful daughters, Allison and Jillian. We visited Mt. Zion UMC in East Cobb, which had a new gym. Two years later, I started a basketball program and poured my energy into it for the next twelve years. It was great seeing the program grow and packing the sanctuary on basketball Sunday. But my focus was too much about personal achievement and not enough about helping young people know Christ.

I continued to live a self-centered life and could go for days without communicating with God. But in 2001, I watched the ESPN Classic special about basketball star Pete Maravich, my idol throughout high school, college, and adulthood. My vintage Maravich jersey hung in my closet for twenty-five years. I bought throwback jerseys, books, and videos on eBay. One VHS tape was Pete's testimony that I watched one Sunday night out of boredom and curiosity. That video was a divine appointment. At the time,

I was drifting away from the basketball program and was very unhappy with myself. I was so far from God after many years of living without him. Jesus on the cross? It was just a story until I heard Pete tell how Christ transformed him. I always wanted to be like Pete, but I realized I wasn't because Jesus Christ knew Pete Maravich, and Jesus didn't know me. Occasionally, I wondered during sermons, *Am I going to heaven?* Then I would fool myself by falling back on my good works. But I knew that if I died that evening, I would never see Jesus face-to-face. I cried out in my heart that I wanted my life to change. As my former pastor, Steve Lyle, often said, "It's not the words you pray as much as the attitude of your heart."

God has blessed me with many opportunities to share my testimony. At first, I was sure I had it all figured out, but instead, there was so much to learn. God led me to turn that basketball program into our Christ-centered Hoops2Heaven ministry. I eventually allowed him to change me in the workplace when I went through trying times after a merger. An opportunity came to teach high school Sunday school and lead the basketball ministry again, which led to the start of a year-round youth sports ministry at Mt. Zion. Can you see a pattern? Youth sports ministry is my fishing hole. I continue to pray that I can get it right for Christ for our families at Mt. Zion and in our community. God loved me unconditionally, wooed me, and showed me mercy time after time until I repented, which means that I turned from my sinful ways, trusted, and obeyed. Repent, trust, and obey. There is no other way. I'm far from perfect, but God thinks I'm worth it. I was lost and then found and forgiven.

BK01
THE HUMAN ERASER AND
THE HUMAN SIN ERASER

Hebrews 10:17, Psalm 103:12

He has taken our sins away from us, as far as the east is from the west.

Psalm 103:12 (NCV)

The late Marvin Webster was an All-American center at tiny Morgan State University in Maryland. He later played professionally for the Seattle Sonics and the New York Knicks and helped lead the Sonics to the NBA Finals in 1978. Marvin played center, stood seven feet tall, and had an enormous wingspan. He was so adept at blocking shots, sometimes achieving triple doubles in rebounds, points, and blocks, that he was nicknamed "the human eraser." Marvin erased shots around the basket with such efficiency that his opponents were often intimidated.

It is noteworthy that Marvin was often seen with a Bible in his hand. Marvin's nickname reminds us of another great eraser. That eraser is Jesus Christ, whom we could call the human sin eraser. Through repentance and confession of our sins and trust in Jesus as Savior and Lord, we can have all of our sins erased as if they had never happened. As humans, we are not capable of forgetting all of the wrongs that others have committed against us. But God assures us that he will not only forgive but forget all of the times we have lied, stolen, made ourselves God, worshiped idols, and taken his name in vain. When we earnestly repent of our sins and place our trust in Christ, a supernatural event occurs. It is as if our sins were written in wax, but the wax melted and eliminated any records of our sins. Where else can we possibly receive such freedom from our past wrongdoings? Only through Jesus Christ, the human sin eraser who erased our sins on the cross, and God, Our Father, who forgives and forgets all of our sins, removing them as far as the east is from the west.

Prayer: Father God, thank you for sending the human sin eraser, Jesus Christ, to wash us as pure as snow with his crimson blood that he shed on the cross for me. Thank you for forgiving and forgetting my sins. In Jesus's holy name. Amen.

BK02
DON'T BE A BALL HOG!

Mark 9:35

> Anyone wanting to become the greatest must become the least, the servant of all. (TLB)

One season I was blessed with an exceptionally talented team of age nine to ten girls in our Hoops2Heaven basketball ministry. The goal is to distribute the talent as evenly as possible, but this particular season, I received more than my fair share of scorers. And scoring was exactly what most of them had in mind. I had at least four players who were capable of scoring double digits on any given day. But it was like breaking young colts to get them to pass the ball. I even tried a scrimmage where the only option to move the ball down the court was to pass with no dribbling. "No dribbling? That's hard! It's not fair!" they screamed. But they learned to move the ball quickly as a result of that drill.

I reminded them on several occasions that there is no *I* in *team*. After practice, I asked, "Now why did we do that drill tonight with no dribbling?" I expected to hear the no *I* in *team* line, but Katie quickly spoke up. "So we won't be a bunch of ball hogs!" I was satisfied that they got it, and I never brought it up again.

We're born to be a bunch of ball hogs. When things don't go our way, from the time we are two years old, we cry out in anger and rebellion. Ever notice that there is no *I* in *team* but that there is an *I* in *sin*, and *pride*, and *selfishness*? Billy Graham once said that most unrighteous anger stems from selfishness. There is only one way to remove the selfishness, and that is to turn from our self-centeredness and trust in Christ as we try to follow his way. Sure, Christ got angry, but it was righteous anger that was directed toward wrongdoing of his fellow man every time. Oftentimes, as Christians, we try so hard to conceal righteous anger that we stand and allow injustices to take place right before our eyes and we do nothing. I've been guilty more times than I care to admit.

There is no *I* in *trust*, *obey*, *love*, *mercy*, and *grace*. As we learn to act on righteous anger and stifle unrighteous anger, we will exhibit more and more Christlike traits. Then we won't remain a bunch of ball hogs. We will become better team players for God's kingdom.

Prayer: Father God, through the Holy Spirit living in me, please let me know when you see me being a ball hog, when I am much more concerned about myself than others. May I learn from concrete experiences so that I have fewer childish outbursts that dishonor Christians and your holy name. In the precious name of Jesus. Amen.

BK03
THE MIRACLE OF KRAIG'S
GAME-WINNING THREE

2 Samuel 9:1–13, Philippians 4:13

I can do all things through Christ who strengthens me.

Philippians 4:13

God blessed our youth sports ministry at Mt. Zion richly when he brought us a teenager named Kraig. He has as much passion for basketball as anybody in our ministry. Kraig was born several months prematurely, and the doctors predicted he would not live. He lived, but the doctors predicted he would never walk. Kraig walked, but the doctors predicted that he would not play basketball. He is a fierce competitor who doesn't let any obstacles deter him from competing and enjoying the game. Kraig plays and plays well even though some jump a little higher and run a little faster.

One Saturday afternoon, I coached a memorable game in the gym at Mt. Zion. This game was especially well played, and our team fought back from a twelve-point second half deficit. Kraig had already hit three three-pointers to bring us back. Kraig's team was down by two points with only five seconds remaining, and the opponents had the basketball. The inbounds pass flew past the top of the key, and one of our players, D'Andre, leaped and made a fantastic one-handed interception. Then D'Andre had the presence of mind to turn and find Kraig on the wing about twenty-five feet from the basket. Kraig let it fly. As the horn sounded, the ball hit nothing but net. We won! Kraig raced to the other end of the court as his mom, dad, and sister leaped out of their seats at mid-court. Kraig's teammates pummeled him with congratulations for the winning shot.

I told my Sunday school class about the winning play the next day, and there were several tears in the room, including mine. That miracle shot was a bright and shining moment, a tribute to the faith of his parents, who kept telling their son that he could do more than the doctors thought he could do. The following Monday evening, I began to prepare my Sunday school lesson about David searching for any member of Jonathan's family to join him. I received an e-mail from Kraig's mother, who described the obstacles that Kraig had overcome since birth. I then understood how special that shot was. Tears filled my eyes again. Then I said, "Oh my!" when I found out my lesson was about Mephibosheth. When King David searched for anyone from Jonathan's family to honor his covenant with Jonathan, his servant, Ziba, could only find young Mephibosheth, who could not run as fast nor jump as high as the others. Although Mephibosheth was not as physically capable as others, he had a humble heart. Because of his father's legacy, God rewarded Mephibosheth with plenty of servants and a permanent seat at King David's table in Jerusalem.

What a great and wonderful God we serve, whose perfect timing surpasses anything we can create.

Prayer: Father God, thank you for the inspiration that you sent us in the form of Kraig and the living witness he has become for all of us who are fortunate to call him son, friend, and brother in Christ. In Jesus's name. Amen.

BK04
WHAT MAKES A TEAM A TEAM?

Romans 12:3–8

Having different gifts according to the grace that is given us…

Romans 12:6

Great teams are characterized by an excellent coach and talented, unselfish players who work as one toward a common goal. Oftentimes, there will be one outstanding player who involves his teammates very effectively, helping them play better than they would otherwise. Larry Bird and Magic Johnson, who were two of the biggest NBA stars in the 1980s, are two players who were strong leaders and brought out the best in their teammates. They were both capable of scoring many points but would pass the ball often to their teammates to get them more involved. Larry and Magic offered encouragement and constructive criticism as necessary. In turn, their teammates would show appreciation by playing even harder to win the game.

The first and second laws of the Ten Commandments teach us not to put our selfish interests above God or even equal with God. In a game, if you don't listen to your coach and instead try to do it all yourself, you will not be successful. If you try to do it yourself by hogging the ball, dribbling through three or four defenders, and taking the first shot you see from twenty-five feet, you will most likely fail, and you'll steal the joy of the game away from your teammates. But if you are centered on listening to your coach, understand what is best for your team, and play your role on the team, you will be more successful.

Some of us are good shooters, some are good passers, some defend well, and some rebound well. Find out what you are good at and focus on that strength for your team. In the early church, Paul taught that some are good at preaching, some are good at serving others, and some are good at teaching. The church is made up of many parts, and when each of us uses the special gifts that God has given us, we add to the overall effectiveness of our respective churches. If you will try to do what your coach (Jesus) teaches you and strive to help others (Mom, Dad, your siblings, and friends), you will live a more joyful life.

Remember the following pecking order in sports: coach, teammates, you. Here is the pecking order in life: Jesus, others, you. Jesus, others, you makes an acronym called JOY. When the joy gets sucked out of your life, it's usually because you've reversed the order and put yourself first before God and Jesus and helping others.

Prayer: Father God, may I find joy knowing that Jesus paid the penalty for my sins by hanging on the cross, no matter what happens to me today. In Jesus's holy and precious name. Amen.

BK05
PETE MARAVICH:
LOOKING UNTO JESUS

Hebrews 12:2, James 4:14, Philippians 1:20–21

Looking unto Jesus, the author and finisher of our faith…

Hebrews 12:2

The last day of Pete Maravich's life on this earth was January 5, 1988. Pete arrived at the Church of the Nazarene gym in Pasadena, California, to play three-on-three basketball with Dr. James Dobson, associate pastor Gary Lydic, former UCLA star Ralph Drollinger, and several friends who were eager to play basketball with the Pistol. Pete had not played basketball for months because of a sore shoulder. On the way to the gym from his hotel, Pete excitedly told Gary how God had changed him and was working in his life. Pete was in California to supervise the shooting of a movie about his boyhood life. The day before Pete left for California, he told his brother in Christ, John Lotz, that all he really wanted to do was travel across the country and tell young people how Jesus Christ had saved him and how they needed Christ in their lives.

But everything changed that morning. After a few half-court games of three-on-three, the players took a water break. Pete was shooting the ball and talking to Dobson, and Lydic was shagging balls for Pete. He told Dobson how much he loved playing basketball that morning for the first time in months. Pete's final words were, "I feel great." Suddenly, Pete collapsed and hit the floor hard face first. At first, Dr. Dobson and Gary Lydic thought he was pulling a prank. Despite twenty minutes of CPR, Pete died in the arms of Dr. Dobson in the gym.

Dobson later recalled that the T-shirt Pete was wearing the moment he went to be with the Lord bore the following words: "Looking unto Jesus."

If you die tonight, will you be looking unto Jesus, the author and finisher of our faith? God only gives us this day. Live it to the fullest, and if you haven't made Christ your Savior, I ask you, "What are you waiting on?"

Prayer: Most gracious and loving Father, help me realize that I need to live each day to the fullest for you because you give us today. Your mercies are new every morning. In Jesus's name. Amen.

BK06
SPORTSMANSHIP FOR THE AGES

Romans 8:26

The Holy Spirit helps us with our daily problems and in our praying. (TLB)

My father, Lester Farr Sr., won over eight hundred games in his high school coaching career that spanned five decades from the 1930s through the 1970s. Dad won one state championship and thirteen region championships and positively influenced the lives of hundreds of young men and women with his strong Christian character, determination, coaching skill, and strong sense of fair play. Coach Farr is ninety-eight and in good health. In fact, he has completed a loop since he was born in the tens and is now living in the tens. Despite the success that he had, he will recall the games that he lost and what he should have done differently more often than the thrilling wins.

At state tournament time each year, I am reminded that strange things happen under the bright lights and the cauldron of tournament pressure. Dad's sense of fair play was most evident in the 1952 state tournament in Macon. His Cedar Grove girls' team won the state championship in 1951 and had a great opportunity to repeat as champions. Cedar Grove trailed by one point in the final seconds when a bizarre play occurred. Following a timeout, the official incorrectly awarded the ball to Cedar Grove when the opponent should have inbounded the ball. The Cedar Grove forward drove to the basket and scored to put her team ahead. Only then did the officials realize that something was wrong.

Somewhat confused, the officials walked over to my dad and asked him what they should do. In the heat of the battle, Coach Farr surely must have thought, *You figure out the mess you made!* There was no correctable error rule in 1952 that would have reversed the points on the board. But Dad told the officials that it would be all right to take the points off the board as long as the clock was reset with the same amount of time. The opponent inbounded the ball and ran out the clock to win the game, ending Cedar Grove's chance for a repeat.

The following morning, *Macon Telegraph* sportswriter Sam Glickman wrote that Coach Farr's willingness to do the right thing, especially considering the circumstances and what was at stake for his team, was one of the finest acts of sportsmanship he had ever witnessed. It was an act of sportsmanship that surely carried over into the lives of the girls who played in the game and their friends and families who watched that evening.

Prayer: Dear Heavenly Father, thank you for the legacy of Coach Farr and his integrity and for coaches everywhere who leave legacies that glorify you. In Jesus's name, I pray. Amen.

BK07
SNOOKS

Romans 2:6–10, Galatians 6:9

But glory, honor, and peace, to every man that works good…

Romans 2:10

My father-in-law, Damon Ray, or Ray as he was affectionately known throughout Hardin County, Kentucky, was a coach and principal at East Hardin High School in Glendale for many years. The school is adjacent to the football stadium, which is named Damon Ray Field. Ray passed away in May 2008, and the funeral service was very appropriately held in the gym at East Hardin High School where he was so beloved.

Although the Glendale schools had been integrated since 1956, in 1963, integration was still making its way through the South. The East Hardin High School boys' basketball team had one African American player, a young sophomore nicknamed "Snooks" Freeman. On a Friday afternoon, East Hardin traveled to Cookeville, Tennessee, to play the Tennessee Tech college freshman team on Saturday afternoon. The team would then stay overnight, play their game, and stay to watch their former classmate compete in the varsity game. But an unfortunate event occurred Friday evening. When the team checked into the hotel, the hotel proprietor told Ray that Snooks could not stay at the hotel, and that he would have to stay at a motel outside of town by himself. Ray was furious, and that evening, Ray drove his daughter, Becca, and his wife, Charlene, to Livingston, Tennessee, to stay with Becca's grandmother. And Ray brought Snooks with them.

The next day, Ray told John Oldham, the Tennessee Tech head coach, about the incident. Oldham assured him that the problem would be taken care of right away, and all of the boys were allowed to stay in the hotel on Saturday night. In another demonstration of Christian love, Oldham invited Ray and his team to his Sunday school class on Sunday morning, including Snooks. When Ray passed away, I spoke with Snooks Freeman at the funeral home. I'm confident that one reason Snooks came was because of the Christian love that Ray showed him.

The Bible assures us that we are all alike in God's eyes. "Neither Jew nor Greek, neither slave nor master …"

All have the same birthright and privilege to come to know Christ. Every person on the face of this earth has had his or her sins paid for by the One who took our places upon the cross. And nobody, regardless of sex, race, or creed, will be denied heaven if that person places his or her faith in Jesus Christ as Savior and Lord.

Prayer: Father God, please teach me to love and respect everyone for who he or she is, regardless of their nationality, heritage, or the color of the person's skin. In Jesus's name. Amen.

BK08
TRIPLE THREAT

Acts 1:1–8, John 14:26, Romans 8:26

But the Helper, the Holy Spirit, whom the Father will send in My name, He will teach you all things, and bring to your remembrance all things that I have said to you.

John 14:26

One of the most important fundamental skills for a basketball player is the triple-threat position. The player crouches in an athletic position with weight on the balls of the feet, which are spread slightly wider than shoulder width. The player holds the basketball firmly and tucked near the body. From this position, the player can jump and shoot, pass the ball, or dribble and drive to the basket. Those are the three options: dribble, pass, and shoot. If you watched the movie *Hoosiers*, when Jimmy made the winning basket, Jimmy was in the triple threat position before he dribbled, leaped, and scored. All expert players have mastered this fundamental skill.

Do you realize that as a child of God, you have a triple threat, the Holy Trinity, at your call every day of your life on earth? First, there is our almighty God, the Father, the maker of the universe, all powerful, all loving, who will never leave nor forsake you. Second, there is Jesus Christ, the Son of God and the Son of Man, who was born to a virgin, walked among us on earth, taught us and performed miracles. Jesus was crucified and suffered an excruciating death on the cross, but he beat the sting of death by rising from the grave on the third day. Jesus now sits at the right hand of the Father, and Jesus intercedes for you when you pray to God. Third, there is the most overlooked and most misunderstood member of the Holy Trinity triple threat, the Holy Spirit. When you receive Christ as your Savior, you are immediately and supernaturally infused with the Holy Spirit, a person living inside you. As you seek to obey God each day, the Holy Spirit helps you with your daily problems and helps you pray, even when you have no clue what to pray for or how to pray. The Holy Spirit passionately fills the prayer gaps for you so that God will understand your prayers even when you don't feel like they made sense.

Each member of the Trinity loves you more than you can ever imagine. Always remember that with the triple threat Trinity over you, by your side, and living within you, all things are possible.

Prayer: Father God, what a blessing it is to have your unconditional love. Thank you for sending your Son, Jesus, to die for me. I am grateful for the gift of the Holy Spirit to help me with my daily problems and to pray. In Jesus's name. Amen.

BK09
REPEAT OR REPENT?

Mark 1:15, Matthew 4:17

For the Kingdom of God is at hand. Repent...

Mark 1:15

When a team wins a championship, its fan base usually celebrates enthusiastically for several days. Then the question begins. Can you repeat next year? Fans don't even give teams a chance to enjoy it before clamoring for more. Fan is short for fanatic. Repeat means the team would win the championship again next year, making it two years in a row. Then if the team wins two in a row, the fans shout, "Three-peat! Three-peat!" or three in a row.

The term "three-peat" was first coined by Los Angeles Laker Byron Scott when he spoke of bringing the Laker fans three consecutive titles. In fact, Laker Coach Pat Riley later licensed the catch phrase. Ironically, the Lakers did not three-peat the following year. The next team to three-peat after the phrase was invented was the Chicago Bulls. In the late 1950s and 1960s, the Boston Celtics "eight-peated" with eight consecutive titles.

How about you? Have you ever repeated or three-peated or one hundred-peated or gazillion-peated an evil action or thought? The same sin, that is. Maybe you've taken God's name in vain or lied or made yourself out to be God or put your interests ahead of others because you think it's all about you. Either you can't shake the sin or you don't want to shake it. The Bible reminds us that there is pleasure in sin. But in the end, you need to realize that the bitterness and destruction is never worth the temporary pleasure.

Do you know that God is angry each day with unrepentant sinners who repeat the same sins over and over? Pray now that God will help you recognize specific sin and that the Holy Spirit will lead you in such a way that you will *repent* and not repeat. Just changing that one little letter from *a* to *n* makes all the difference. Turn from the sinful self that binds you and break the chains of repeat sin. Cleanse yourself through the blood of the Lamb, Jesus Christ.

Prayer: Father God, help me repent, not repeat. Show me when I mess up so that I will turn from that sin and not do it again. Please forgive me when I fall short. In Jesus's name. Amen.

BK10
KEEP YOURSELVES FROM
(AMERICAN) IDOLS,
LITTLE CHILDREN

1 John 5:21, Romans 3:23

Little children, keep yourselves from idols. Amen.

1 John 5:21

Many young athletes have a favorite player, a player he or she looks up to because the player is one of the best in that sport. In basketball today, two of the most popular players are Lebron James and Kobe Bryant, often referred to simply as Lebron and Kobe. My idol for many years was Pete Maravich. I rightly call him an idol because he was just that to me, much bigger and more important than God was in my life. If Pete had a great game, I was ecstatic because I knew people would say and write great things about him. If he had a bad game, I was disconsolate and moody. I admired Pete and wanted to be like him because he had these great skills and was very cool. But Pete admitted that he was no role model during his playing days because of his drinking and lifestyle. My acts of idolatry included growing a goatee like Pete, buying a jersey like Pete's, running like Pete, and trying to pass and shoot like Pete. I quit being myself and tried to be somebody else.

If you have put an athlete on a pedestal, you are in a dangerous position. Eventually, that athlete will do something to let you down because the athlete is human. All people have sinned and fallen short of the glory of God. All people are imperfect and will eventually fall short and disappoint you. Pray that God will give you a proper perspective to enjoy the athlete's performance but never put the athlete on a pedestal or make the athlete a god in your life. The Bible teaches that placing people on pedestals is sinful because that's when you put them above God. Know where to draw the line. If you find yourself way down because an athlete or team lost, then you might have lost perspective. The ability to maintain proper perspective is one of the wonderful benefits of being a child of God. If you are a believer, the Holy Spirit will help you maintain balance and perspective the next time your favorite athlete does something great or throws a bad interception.

Prayer: Father God, thank you for what I can learn from great athletes and the ways that I can enjoy their performances. Help me realize that only you are to be placed on a pedestal, your throne. In Jesus's holy name. Amen.

BK11
THE MIRACLE IN
THE GEORGIA DOME

Hebrews 1:12, 13:8; James 1:17

But you are the same, and your years will not fail.

Hebrews 1:12

I was in the Georgia Dome for the 2008 SEC Basketball Championship the night a tornado hit and witnessed the miracle shot only minutes before the building shook. At noon that day, in a pouring rainstorm, I scrounged three tickets downtown so that Becca, Allison, and I could see our beloved Kentucky Wildcats. The first game in the evening session was Alabama and Mississippi State. With one second remaining in regulation and Bama down by three, Mykal Riley hit a twenty-four-foot shot to send the game into overtime. But it was the way the ball went in the basket that earned the nickname "the miracle shot." The ball rattled around, hit the backboard, hit the front iron, teetered, and finally fell in. Last-second shots just don't do that. It was as if God tipped in the shot to send the game to OT.

Ten minutes later, the players on the court backed away from the north side of the court, staring at the ceiling as the tornado brushed the Georgia Dome. The sound was like the classic freight train. It appeared that giant animals were making paw prints all over the fabric roof of the dome. I stood transfixed, watching debris fall from the roof, as Becca and Allison yelled at me to move for safe cover.

There is universal agreement that Riley's shot saved many lives that evening. If Riley's shot didn't go in, hundreds of Alabama fans would have headed immediately for the exits to make the drive to Alabama. You don't hang around at tournaments when your team gets eliminated. That departure would have put them directly in the path of a 130-mile-per-hour twister because there was no warning from Georgia Dome event management.

God is still in the miracle business because he never changes. Hebrews 13:8 tells us that Jesus Christ is the same yesterday, today, and forever. God speaks to people through modern-day miracles. God might use different approaches in the twenty-first century because there was no game called basketball two thousand years ago. So his ways change, but what will never change is his desire to see everyone come to know Jesus Christ. That's why he has been so patient, giving everyone an opportunity to know Jesus before he comes back. In heaven, I believe that the saints will know the impact of God's mercy on his kingdom through the Georgia Dome miracle, God's wake-up call to the twenty-five thousand in attendance that evening.

Prayer: Most gracious and merciful God, thank you for the modern-day miracles that affect lives for eternity. In Jesus's name. Amen.

BK12
PILGRIMAGE TO BATON ROUGE

John 14:6

I am the Way, the Truth, and the Life. No one comes to the
Father except through Me.

On November 2, 2003, I dedicated my life to Jesus Christ at the
age of forty-eight after watching a VHS tape of a testimony by
Pete Maravich. I received God's free gift of grace and eternal life
in heaven. Only six weekends prior, Becca, Allison, Jillian, and I
traveled to Baton Rouge for the LSU-UGA football game. It was
my first trip ever to Baton Rouge, and I was thrilled to walk inside
the Cow Palace, also known as the John W. Parker Ag Center, and
imagine what it was like to be in an overflow crowd watching Pete
go for another fifty. Allison and I walked by Tiger Stadium to the
Pete Maravich Assembly Center, named for Pete shortly after his
death in 1988, and took some photos as some LSU fans razzed us.
I knew Pete was in heaven and how he came to know Christ, but I
was so into me that I rarely thought about my future and my eternity. It is still amazing to me how God used Pete's testimony on
a VHS tape to bring me to Christ in my den only six weeks later.

Fast forward five years to October 2008, and it was time
for Georgia to visit LSU again on the five-year SEC schedule
rotation. I just had to go back. How different my life was then,
but I still needed to grow so much. That summer, I became

spiritually lazy and rested on my laurels after spearheading our first church golf tournament, Golf for His Glory. As I stood in my closet one afternoon, the thought hit me that Pete had died five years after becoming a Christian. Here I was approaching the fifth anniversary of being a Christian, and I hadn't done squat for Christ lately. It was a real wake-up call, and I prayed that my trip to Baton Rouge this time would honor God and be one of spiritual renewal.

On a picture-perfect Friday, I left Becca in New Orleans and drove to the LSU campus. I received a personal tour of the Maravich Center from the operations manager and thoroughly enjoyed seeing Pete's memorabilia in Pete Maravich Pass, dedicated to Pete's memory in 2007. I walked throughout the Cow Palace, even down in the bowels of what is now a rodeo facility. Finally, I went out to Resthaven Gardens in East Baton Rouge to pay homage to the man God used to bring me to Christ. I knelt at Pete's marker, read John 14 silently, talked to God, and gave God the glory for using Pete to save me. Later, I thought, *Who will one day visit my grave and thank me for leading them to Christ?*

Who will one day kneel at your grave and thank you? When we get to heaven, I believe one of the coolest things will be to see the amazing tapestry that God has woven as he has chosen to use flawed human beings to advance his kingdom. I believe we will get to see our spiritual tree and celebrate with those who came before us and will come after us.

Prayer: Heavenly Father, thank you for the Christian legacy of Peter Press Maravich and the events that you use in my daily life to draw me closer to you so that I can enjoy a life that is dedicated to the kingdom of God. In Jesus's name. Amen.

BK13
RECEIVING MERCY...
FROM A REFEREE?

Lamentations 3:22–26, 32; Philippians 1:6

His mercies are new every morning…

Lamentations 3:23

When you are a new basketball player, it's difficult to learn and obey all of the rules. If the referee called every rules violation that players committed, the game would be 2–0 or 4–2. That game would not be much fun to play, nor would it be much fun to watch. The referee should always call violations such as running with the ball, three seconds, double dribble, and fouls when a clear advantage is gained illegally by a player. Hard, physical fouls need to be called to keep players safe and lessen the chance of injury. The referee actually shows you *mercy* by not penalizing you when you make mistakes as you learn to play the game and protects you from injury by controlling the physical play in the game.

You should be very thankful that God also shows you mercy when you are a new Christian. Even though you become a Christian, you still have many years before you become a mature Christian. God wants to encourage you, especially in your first few years. If God called you out on every sin and gave you the full measure that you deserve, you could become very discouraged and never get off the starting line. When we are baby Christians, God will correct us through the Holy Spirit but not discipline us as severely as he will years later. The longer that we have been Christians, the higher his expectations are for us to live a life that is perfect in Christ. So if you are a fairly new Christian, like a toddler, God will give you some cool surprises to encourage your walk and to keep you excited and motivated about growing as a Christian. Praise God that he knows exactly what each of us needs to grow in love and obedience.

Prayer: Father God, thank you for your mercy and compassion, and for not giving me the full measure of what I deserve when I break your rules. In Jesus's name. Amen.

BK14
THE GREATEST 360 IN HISTORY

Mark 15:25–37

It was the third hour, and they crucified him… at the ninth hour Jesus cried with a loud voice…

Mark 15:25, 37

One of the most dramatic, athletic, and thrilling plays in basketball is a breakaway 360 slam dunk. A 360 dunk means that the player leaves his feet while facing the basket, goes high into the air, and rotates his body a full 360 degrees or one complete revolution before slamming the ball home. Many players have mastered this move, and fans will debate which athlete has been the best at the 360. When I asked my players at open gym one night about the greatest 360 dunk they had seen, one young man named Jullian said without hesitation, "Vince Carter at the All-Star game [Toronto, 2000]." Still others mentioned Kobe Bryant. And from a generation ago, I told them about Dominique Wilkins, the Atlanta Hawks star who was nicknamed the human highlight film because of his spectacular dunks and aerial maneuvers. Whoever executes a 360 dunk causes the fans to go crazy and spill their popcorn in celebration.

After I asked our players who the greatest 360 dunker was, I asked them to tell me the greatest 360 in history—not just in basketball or in sports, but in history. None of them followed me, so I read them two verses from the book of Mark. The first verse said simply that Jesus Christ was crucified at nine in the morning. The second verse stated that the skies turned black from noon to 3:00 p.m., at which time Jesus declared, "It is finished," and gave up his spirit. Jesus hung on the cross for you and me from 9:00 a.m. to 3:00 p.m. Let's do the math. Six hours times sixty minutes per hour is *360 minutes*. The greatest 360 in history is because of what the cross and the demonstration of love meant for mankind. Jesus didn't just drink from the cup. He drained it and tasted every drop of sin that will ever be committed. As if to make a point, because prophetically he could have come down well before then, he hung and hung and hung to show Satan, "Who's your daddy now?" Jesus showed his amazing love for us by continuing to pull himself up to draw one more breath, raking his torn and bleeding back against the splinters on the cross for 360 minutes, the greatest 360 there ever was, is, and is to come.

Prayer: Dear Jesus Christ, what an incredible gift of love you gave me when you hung a 360 on the rugged cross for me. In Jesus's name. Amen.

BK15
THE NEXT TIME I SEE PISTOL

Philippians 1:20–21

For to me, to live is Christ, and to die is gain.

Philippians 1:21

I vividly recall the last time that I saw Pete Maravich, and it was the closest that I had ever physically been to him. The scene was the old Omni Arena in Atlanta in 1980. The Hawks had just defeated the Celtics on a last-second shot by Eddie Johnson. Pete had played sparingly in his backup role with the Celtics, and the biggest reaction that night had been to his new perm 'do and the rainbow layups he kissed off the glass during warm-ups. Even in a backup role, Pete enthralled his legion of fans.

After the game, my friend, Joel, and I went down to the dressing room to get another glimpse of Pete. I looked up and Pete was standing by the wall, talking to a group of admirers and friends. Joel pleaded, "Go on over there! Go meet him." Joel understood perhaps better than anyone my infatuation and idol worship of Pistol. I wanted so desperately to meet him, but I respected his privacy. And what if he rejected me? My biggest fear was that Pete wouldn't react to me like I wanted him to, me, his biggest fan who pressed his ear to a transistor radio and listened to him score sixty-eight against the Knicks and who was shattered when Pete blew out his knee and missed his All-Star homecoming in Atlanta.

I would never see Pistol again. He retired after that season. I met my future wife, Becca, that summer. Georgia won the national championship. We married, and Allison and Jillian were born in 1984 and 1987. I thought of him sparingly over the years and was vaguely aware that Pete had dedicated his life to Christ. On January 5, 1988, I walked in the door from work, and Joel was on the phone. "Did you hear about Pistol? He died of a heart attack in a pickup basketball game today." I said, "You're kidding me. That can't be." Joel said, "You know I wouldn't kid you about that." I was in a bit of shock. I began to reflect as the ESPN sportscast replayed a recent interview with Pete as Pete described the difference that Jesus Christ had made in his life. But it didn't cause me to reflect on my missing relationship with Christ. I had plenty going on with my job, my growing family, and a promising college refereeing career. Sure, I had kept my Pistol number 7 Jazz home jersey in my closet for the past ten years and would keep it for the next fifteen. But who could have known that fifteen years later, I would watch a video tape of Pete's testimony that would draw me to the Son? And now, someday, I will see Pete again. When I enter the pearly gates, maybe he'll hit me with a behind-the-back pass for an easy layup. My dad and Pete's dad, Press, will be there to coach, and my mom will keep score just like she did when my dad coached. Pistol, I can't wait to see you again.

Prayer: Dear Lord, thank you for the legacy of Pistol Pete, which is still bringing people into the kingdom of God. In Jesus's name. Amen.

BK16
HOOPIN' IT UP IN COSTA RICA

Matthew 9:37–38, 28:19–20

Therefore, go and make disciples in all the nations…

Matthew 28:19

The summer after I was saved, I went with a Mt. Zion UMC mission team to Costa Rica. My former pastor, Tom Pilgrim, said that I should go to help me grow, so I went. The personal highlight of the trip was taking about seventy pounds of sports equipment to the Cartago church. In the suitcase were a makeshift wooden backboard, a basketball hoop and net, and some deflated basketballs. One afternoon, my friend, David, and I bolted the backboard and rim to a mahogany post in the dirt-laden church yard and we burned up three drill bits in the process. But once the goal was up there, it wasn't coming down. I figured it would last for two weeks, but two years later, a mission team brought me pictures of the hoop still standing.

As I had hoped, basketball turned out to be a great way to meet the kids from the neighborhood. I have some great pictures of American and Costa Rican kids playing five on five. The dirt court was so black that after minutes of handling the ball, your hands would be pitch black. I became friends with Daniel, Isaac, Kenneth, and the pastor's son, David (pronounced Da-veed). After we played for the final time on a Thursday afternoon, I shared my testimony with the boys and told them all about Pistol Pete Maravich through Eric, our interpreter. But I failed to offer them an opportunity to receive Christ. I still didn't realize that God had blessed me with a story that he could use to change lives. Once I realized that God had blessed me with this special gift, it haunted me for some time that I had not given them this opportunity. The missed opportunity helped me know how important it is to take advantage of chances to share Christ with others as the Holy Spirit leads.

Prayer: Most wonderful Father, give me the discernment and courage to pull the net for your kingdom when the Spirit leads. Give me a heart and a burden for the unsaved. In Jesus's name. Amen.

BK17
CAN YOU TRACE YOUR
ROOTS IN CHRIST?

Acts 2:1–17, Exodus 20:4–6

I will pour out of my Spirit upon all flesh…

Acts 2:17

One evening, I read the story of Henrietta Mears, a wonderful Christian saint who began a Sunday school class in Southern California that reached thousands of people for Christ beginning in the 1930s. Mears started a summer camp in the San Bernardino Mountains for youth, and one young man who came through her camp in 1951 was Bill Bright, who would begin the Campus Crusade for Christ ministry. Bill Bright is given credit for millions of people receiving Christ during his fifty-year ministry through Campus Crusade and his production and distribution of *The Jesus Film*.

One young man who came through Bright's San Bernardino camp in the summer of 1966 was a six-foot-five-inch shooting guard named Pistol Pete Maravich. Perhaps someone sensed that Pete was about to throw away a promising college and pro career through his reckless lifestyle, because Pete received an invitation to put on his *Showtime* clinic at the event. To make a long story short, Pete drove over four thousand miles and never did a clinic.

Instead, he was placed in a small group for three days. When Bright gave the invitation to receive Christ, Pete rejected Jesus and was quite cavalier and defiant about it.

But sixteen years later, when Pete was at his wit's end one night when all of the sins he had committed kept coming up in his mind, he remembered the seeds that had been sown at Bright's camp and the message of salvation. Pete received Christ in November 1982 at the foot of his bed at five thirty in the morning. Three years later, Pete would give a testimony in Phoenix, Arizona, that was taped and became a hot item after Pete died suddenly in 1988.

I bought the testimony tape in 2003 on eBay and was saved after watching it on November 2, 2003. It was a startling and cool revelation to see how Mears to Bright to Maravich to Farr had evolved. Apparently, others have received Christ through my testimony to FCA groups, youth groups, and the youth sports ministry.

I believe one day we will see this amazing believer-ology tree in heaven that will show us the Christian lineage of person after person, generation after generation. We will see the impact that we had on the lives of other believers.

How do you trace your Christian lineage? Was it your father, mother, youth pastor, friend, Sunday school teacher, or VBS volunteer? Perhaps it was a close friend whom you admired or an athlete, as was my case. Do you even have a lineage to trace? Generations of your family will be influenced by the choices you make for or against Christ.

Prayer: Most holy and powerful God, what confidence you had when you trusted twelve ordinary men to carry the torch of salvation after Jesus ascended. May I help continue the lineage that these brave disciples began. In Jesus's name. Amen.

BK18
NEED A FRESH JERSEY?

2 Corinthians 5:17, John 11:25–26, 14:6; 1 John 1:9

The one who lives and believes in Me will never die ever.
Do you believe this?

John 11:26 (HCS)

At our summer basketball camps and league play, some nights, the A/C doesn't work very well. The temperature in the gym can be eighty degrees, which means plenty of sweaty bodies. We use reversible jerseys to move kids between teams so that the games remain competitive. Those sweaty jerseys become stinky jerseys after a couple of nights, especially if the jerseys are thrown into a pile. The next day, if you pick one up and take a good sniff, you might need smelling salts to revive you. By hanging up the jersey and letting it air out, it's not so bad, but the stench is still there. The only way to get a fresh, clean-smelling jersey is to wash it in soapy water. The clean smell returns, and that jersey is worth wearing again. You exchange a stinky, smelly, foul-smelling jersey for a fresh, clean, sweet-smelling jersey.

Before we knew Christ, our life's odor to God was always like that stinky, smelly jersey in the pile for three days. The odor came from the buildup of sin in our lives because we consistently disobeyed his law, which angers God. Don't believe we stink before we are saved? It's true. The only way to get rid of our putrid odor is to be washed clean by the blood of the Lamb. We don't change our lives so much as we *exchange* our old lives for new lives in Christ. Paul made it clear in 2 Corinthians that when someone becomes a Christian, he or she becomes a new person. The old person is out; in with the new.

I heard Paige, a former missionary to the Russian republic of Kazakhstan, share this story that helps illustrate the point. One afternoon, she was on a bus in Kazakhstan, sitting across the aisle from a man whose odor she described as simply repulsive. He had open sores, his hair was dirty, his clothes were filthy, and his odor reeked across the aisle. As she looked at him, she sensed God speaking to her. *What? You don't think your sin is smelly, stinky, and repulsive to me?*

Just as we exchange a filthy jersey for a clean one, we exchange our filthy, sinful nature for one that is pure in Christ. When you turn from sin and place your trust in Christ, immediately you are cleansed by the blood of our precious Savior and given the Holy Spirit. As Jesus works within you, the difference in your new life versus your old life should become as striking as the difference between the putrid jersey and the clean jersey.

You will constantly get ugly stains (sin) on your new jersey. But the way to get rid of them is to spot clean your jersey. Tell God exactly what caused the spot and where the spot is, and together, Jesus and God will cleanse you. First John 1:9: "If we confess our sins, he is faithful and just, and will forgive our sins, and cleanse us from all unrighteousness."

You will stain your new jersey, but you should not retain the stench of your old jersey. If you do, you might be a false convert, having never actually received the Holy Spirit. A false convert hears the Word and gets excited for a while but falls by the wayside when trials and temptations come.

Go ahead and sniff your jersey. Need a fresh one? Jesus is holding a clean number 1 jersey just for you. Jesus said, "I am the

Way, the Truth, and the Life." Jesus is the only way to God and to heaven.

Prayer: Father God, thank you for spot-cleaning me when I confess what I have messed up and for making me as pure as snow again. In Jesus's name. Amen.

BK19
THE FINALS

Matthew 7:21–29

I never knew you. Depart from Me, you who practice lawlessness!

Matthew 7:23

The National Basketball Association calls its championship series The Finals, which pits the Eastern Conference champion against the Western Conference champion. Can you name the winner of the The Finals in 1999? How about 2004? If The Finals were truly final, then perhaps you and I could remember who the champion was. If The Finals were played this year and never played again, we would remember the champion.

The day of judgment is the finals when God returns the verdict on your life. You will either be a big winner or a big loser on that day. There won't be another day of judgment, a second chance or a replay. You will be the biggest winner ever if you repented of your sins and took Jesus as your Savior during this lifetime. When judgment day comes for you, Jesus will act as your intercessor. When you come face to face with God Almighty and are too awestruck to utter your name, Jesus will speak on your behalf and say, "Father, this is [your name]. I know [your name]. Remember that on [date], [your name] repented and accepted me as Savior. I paid the penalty for [your name]'s sins on the cross. I bore those sins in my body on the cross. You remember, right?" When Jesus intercedes for you, God will welcome you to heaven with open and loving arms for all eternity. If you never made that commitment, Jesus will say, "I'm sorry. I never knew [your name]." The Bible promises that there will be weeping, torment, and gnashing of teeth for all eternity.

Prepare for these finals today by repenting of your sins and inviting Christ into your heart. The best time to plant a tree is today. The same goes for determining your salvation for eternity. Today is the best day.

Prayer: Father God, thank you for making Jesus my intercessor to represent me on judgment day. May he recognize me and speak for me, having paid the price for me on the cross for my sin. May I see you both in heaven. In Jesus's name. Amen.

BK20
BEATING THE ODDS

Luke 12:40

So be ready at all times, for I, the Messiah, will come when least expected. (TLB)

If you coach a basketball team, pick your best shooter to shoot a series of shots at practice. Before the player shoots, ask the players how many believe that the player will make a layup. Most, if not all, hands will go up. Have the player shoot the layup. Then repeat the procedure for a ten-footer, a free throw, a three-pointer, a half-court shot, and a seventy-foot desperation heave. Note that fewer hands go up with each shot. I doubt any player will raise his hand seriously for the seventy-footer.

Explain to the players that the odds of receiving Christ are similar to making those shots. The odds of coming to know Christ is much greater in grade school (like the layup and ten-footer), but the odds become increasingly longer in middle school (the free throw), high school (the three-pointer), college (thirty-footer), and adulthood (the half-court or desperation shot).

By the time a person reaches forty to fifty years of age and is not a believer, experts have estimated that less than 10 percent, or one in ten, will become a believer. As unconfessed sin builds up, it hardens your heart like rings on a tree. You become less receptive to the Word and more skilled in your ability to fool yourself, especially if you are leading a successful, comfortable life that appears to reflect your success. Why would you want to mess with good when so many other people around you have it bad? By the way, the odds of making the seventy-foot desperation heave are about the same as a deathbed conversion, probably less than 1 percent. Please don't allow time to run out when eternity is at stake.

The odds are certain that some players on your team or members of your family will never go to heaven. Beat the odds personally by surrendering your life to Christ while you're young. The sooner the better, before the odds become stacked against you.

Prayer: Father God, may I be perfectly in tune with your will and your plan for my life, which includes being in heaven with you one day. Help me understand that the longer I wait the greater the risk that I will be eternally separated from you. In Jesus's name. Amen.

BK21
PISTOL PETE'S BOX SCORE
(PART 1)

Hebrews 10:17, Romans 12:1–2, John 14:6

Do not be conformed…, but be transformed by the renewing of your mind…

Romans 12:2

On February 25, 1977, Pete Maravich scored sixty-eight points on twenty-six field goals and sixteen free throws against the New York Knicks, even though he fouled out with a minute to play. As he left the floor, eleven thousand fans chanted, "Pete! Pete! Pete!" But Pete was a restless, discontented person off the court and showed little joy on the court. He shared that he didn't want to get up the next morning because people would expect sixty-eight again. Sure enough, a CBS TV announcer issued this challenge before his next game: "Pete can prove he is really this good if he scores forty today." Note: Pete had thirty-five at the half and finished with forty-three.

Pistol Pete's Basketball Box Score

Name	FG	FG Attempts	FT	FT Attempts	Assists	Rebounds	Total Score
Maravich	26	43	16	19	5	6	68

But Pete's life box score did not resemble his basketball box score. Pete was not a Christian when he scored sixty-eight. He did not have a relationship with Jesus Christ, although he went to church as a child. When he was a teenager, Pete rejected Christ at a Campus Crusade event in California. Pete thought being a Christian would interfere with his worldly basketball goals. He was defiant and said that Jesus Christ on the cross was "just a story." Pete thought that he was a pretty good guy, that he could do as he pleased so long as he didn't hurt anybody. Although he had a great family with two sons and was a millionaire when a million was a lot of money, he was miserable until Christ became his Savior and Lord.

Your daily box score without Christ could look like this on a typical day.

Helped Poor	Witnessed	Read Bible	Prayed	Meditated	Worshipped	Helped Family	Fellowship
0	0	0	0	0	0	1	0

Prayer: Father God, help me to see where I am making turnovers in my life. Thank you that you encourage me to tell you when I've messed up. You already know anyway, and I thank you that you will always forgive and forget when I sincerely confess my mistakes. In Jesus's name. Amen.

BK22
PISTOL PETE'S BOX SCORE
(PART 2)

Romans 12:2, Colossians 3:17

So that you may prove what is that good and acceptable and perfect will of God.

Romans 12:2

Pete experienced a dramatic transformation in Christ, as evidenced by his deeds and actions. One Thanksgiving, Pete bought a hundred turkeys, and he and his pastor delivered them to the poor families in Baton Rouge. Pete witnessed throughout the United States, and God used him to bring hundreds of people to know Jesus Christ through these talks and his Christian basketball camp in Florida. Pete studied the Bible for hours at a time and became well-versed in scripture. Bible study and prayer were key to Pete's rapid growth and transformation as a Christian because he trained and renewed his mind each day. Del Wubbena, who helped Pete start his Christian basketball camp, once told me, "Pete grew more in five years than any man I have ever known." Pete led his wife and dad to accept Christ. He cared for his dad night and day for six months before Press died of cancer. Pete developed strong relationships with other brothers in Christ. He donated speaking engagement money to nonprofit charities and his church.

Sure, Pete had his weak moments and fell down like we all do. After his conversion, Pete drank a few beers one day, and the next day, he poured the wine from his expensive collection down the kitchen sink. He apologized to people he had hated or he had hurt, even though the circumstances that separated them had happened many years ago. This story is not simply to tell you what a great guy Pete Maravich became. It is to illustrate the greatness of God and Jesus Christ, and turning to Jesus is how amazing transformations begin for Pete, for me, and for you. Your daily box score in Christ could look like this.

Good Deeds in the Name of Christ Box Score

Helped Poor	Witnessed	Read Bible	Prayed	Meditated	Worshipped	Helped Family	Fellow-ship
3	4	2	5	1	1	4	3

Reflect briefly on what your box score looks like so far today. Are your good deeds outweighing the bad ones? The good news is that we are all works in progress. As you grow in Christ, you will become less conscious of your good deeds because they will just evolve naturally from your relationship with Christ. That's what happened to Pistol Pete, and it can happen for you!

Prayer: Dear Father, thank you for what I can learn from the legacy of Pete Maravich, a man who dedicated himself to sharing the gospel with so many people. May I emulate his example of witnessing for you whenever I get the chance. In Jesus's name. Amen.

BK23
BE READY TO COME
OFF THE BENCH

Hebrews 12:1, Luke 12:40

Throw off everything…that so easily entangles us …

Hebrews 12:1 (NIV)

Many times, when the outcome of a game hangs in the balance, the decisive play is not made by the MVP, or the leading rebounder, or even a starter, but by a substitute who comes off the bench. In basketball, there are twelve to fifteen players on a team, but only five can start the game. It's really important that the non-starters pay close attention, study the game, and be ready at all times. You might suddenly be rushed into the game if a player is injured. You might only have a brief opportunity to help the team, and you want to make the most of that chance. If you aren't ready, you won't make the play that your team needs.

As a Christian, sometimes you feel as if you are not in the game for God. Either you've not studied his Word or haven't been in prayer with him lately. Perhaps there is a secret sin that has derailed you temporarily. When the opportunity comes to listen to a friend who needs to vent, or to share Christ when someone opens a door, you miss it like a breakaway layup ahead of the field. The biggest detriment is our attitude, which can be self-centered, especially when sin has separated us from God. Just like a player rips off his warm-ups to enter the game, you must be prepared to "throw off everything [sin] that easily entangles [you]," so you can "run with perseverance the race set before [you]" (Hebrews 12:1).

If you focus on loving God and all the daily blessings he gives you and especially remember the sacrifice that Christ made on the cross for you, then you will want to return his love and be obedient. If you are obedient, you will stay ready and see where God is working. That is where the opportunities to help grow God's kingdom are. Even as insignificant as you might feel, your contributions could make the difference for a friend or family member for eternity. Remember, God chose to operate with twelve very ordinary, challenging, and disparate individuals who changed the world after they received the Holy Spirit. After you have received the Holy Spirit, you are no different from Andrew and Peter. Trust that God can do a mighty work through you, even when you feel like a part-time player.

Prayer: Dear Lord, help me stay true to you so that I'm ready to leap off the bench to make a play for the kingdom of God. In Jesus's name. Amen.

BK24
DO NOT FEAR

Deuteronomy 31:6, Joshua 1:9, Hebrews 13:5

I will never leave you nor forsake you.

Hebrews 13:5

Since my father was a high school coach, and my mother was the scorekeeper, and my older sister, Regina, and older brother, L.E., were outstanding basketball players, I have been in gyms since I was in diapers. I was a gym rat, no question. I have been to state tournaments with Dad's teams and always sat on the bench with him. I have been in big crowds at Atlanta Braves games and was around exciting sports events all of my life. But when I was thirteen and fourteen, panic attacks seized me at ball games. I can remember playing in a region tournament game when I was a sophomore. I was barely five feet tall, and when our guards fouled out, Coach Lake had no choice but to play me. I was so nervous that I was fighting for my breath, and I was probably hyperventilating. Somehow, I managed to get through the game. In fact, I stole a pass in overtime that helped us win the game. A local sportswriter described the steal as having been made by "Danny Farr, at four feet eleven inches, the smallest high school player in the state of Georgia." Man was I embarrassed. A similar anxiety attack had happened at the boys' first round game at state the previous year and at the girls' state tournament. There was no reason for it. Eventually, the bad feelings passed, and I haven't had a problem since.

Those episodes made me reflect on why I was fearful. I had nothing to fear. How much better off I would have been if I had gone to God and asked him to help me? But Christ was not part of my life, even though I had that great opportunity to receive him as my Savior when I was thirteen. The Bible tells us 365 times not to fear, once for each day of the year. "Do not be afraid…for the Lord your God is with you wherever you go" (Joshua 1:9). All you need to do is "draw near to God, and God will draw near to you" (James 4:8) and protect you. How I wish that I had realized back then that the Lord my God was with me wherever I went to guide me and protect me. He will take you through your difficult situations if you let him. As a believer, I have no reason to fear man, and no matter what happens on this earth, my eternity in heaven is assured. What a comforting thought for Christians.

Prayer: Dear Lord God Almighty, when I am fearful, please remind me that you are there to lead me, guide me, hold me, and protect me from harm. In Jesus's holy name. Amen.

BK25
THE NAIL AT THE
FREE-THROW LINE

Luke 23:32–34, Isaiah 53:1–5, Psalm 22:16

By His stripes we are healed.

Isaiah 53:5

On many basketball courts, a single nail is driven at each end of the court to mark the exact center of the free-throw line. That spot is exactly six feet from either side of the free-throw lane line. When a player shoots a free throw, a player carefully aligns at a perfect ninety-degree angle with the front of the rim. The shooter ensures that the forearm is exactly perpendicular to the basket so that the odds of making the shot are the greatest. The release and follow through should point directly toward the front of the rim. The greater the angle the tougher the shot. When the player places one foot directly behind the nail, the player *knows* that he or she is centered perfectly, and the player's confidence level increases.

You and I need to be perfectly aligned with Christ and place him at the exact center of our lives. You center Christ in your life when all aspects of your life are under his guidance. Remember that Christ took the nails for you and me so that we could be freed from the control of sin in our lives, and we could choose to receive the free gift of eternal life in heaven. Remember how Jesus took a nail through his feet that was driven into the wooden cross? He was pierced for your sin and mine. To be Christ-centered, you must truly turn from all of your sins, place your trust in Jesus, obey him daily by reading the Word, being in prayer, and truly worship God.

The next time you shoot a free throw, look down to see if someone drove a nail into the wood for you so that you could find the center of the free throw line. Let that nail remind you to stay Christ-centered on and off the court.

Prayer: Dear Father God, when I use my hands and feet today, I will give thanks that Jesus took the nails in his hands and feet for me so that I could be free to live from the clutches of sin. Help me stay centered in Christ today. In Jesus's name. Amen.

BK26
FIX YOUR EYES ON THE TARGET

Hebrews 12:2

Looking unto Jesus, the author and finisher of our faith...

I asked a group of basketball campers where they aim when they shoot. The replies came back quickly: "The basket," "The backboard." The backboard? Why not just aim at the back wall. Their aims weren't specific at all. I explained that it is very important for a shooter to pick a specific point at which to aim. When I shoot a free throw, I pick out the eyelet (the hook that holds the net strand) on the very front of the rim. Then I try to drop the ball over the eyelet into the basket. The eyelet gives me a very specific aim point.

If you shoot an arrow at a target, do you aim at the entire circle or at the bull's eye? If you want a car or your bicycle to go straight, you pick out a spot in the distance and the car or bike just seems to go to that spot. Take your eye off the spot, and the car or bike drifts left or right.

That's how it is with maintaining focus in your life. If you look here and then over there and then somewhere else for answers and for direction, you'll be all over the map. Hebrews 12:2 teaches us to keep our eyes on Jesus, who is the author (Creator) and finisher of our faith. If you stay focused daily on Jesus, you won't be wandering here and there, searching for answers. Jesus is the only answer to the most important question that matters. How do I get to heaven? If you stay focused on Jesus and seek his guidance, you will eventually discern the unique plan that God has made for you. A key ingredient of the plan is your inborn passion. Everybody has a passion for something. The key is finding it and then channeling that passion for Christ. You don't know how? Keep your eye on Jesus and the Holy Spirit living within you, and God will do the rest. When you look at Jesus, you can know that your future is safe.

Keep your eye on the eyelet of the rim, and keep your eyes on Jesus, who endured the cross and scorned its shame just for you.

Prayer: Dear Father God, help me stay focused each and every hour of each and every day on Jesus. When I fall short, please forgive me. In Jesus's holy and precious name. Amen.

BK27
DON'T BECOME DISTRACTED

Luke 9:62

Anyone who allows himself to be distracted from the work
that I plan for him is not fit for the Kingdom of God. (TLB)

As a boy, Pistol Pete Maravich practiced basketball eight to ten
hours a day in the summer in sweltering, empty gyms. One summer day, he began to cry while sitting in the floor of the Clemson
College gym, wondering what possibly drove him to such lengths
when his friends were at the lake. *Why am I here? Why do I have
this desire? Why am I killing myself?* he wondered. But he got up
and resumed one of the forty or fifty ball-handling drills his father and coach, Press, had created for him. Pete wasn't about to
give up his three goals of earning a college scholarship, making a
million dollars, and being a world champion. God made Pete to
be able to concentrate on repetitive tasks for long periods of time.
As Pete mastered the fundamental skills, Press gave him more
complicated drills, which Pete also mastered. He became so good
at the drills that incredible passes, shots, and dribbles became routine. Even though Pete last played in the NBA in 1980, many
experts still consider Pete to be the greatest ball handler, dribbler,
and passer to ever play basketball.

Two years after he retired from professional basketball, Pete
received Christ as his Savior and Lord. He approached his study of

the Bible with the same type of fervor and dedication that rivaled his attention to basketball drills as a child. Pete stayed focused and did not allow himself to be distracted from daily Bible study and prayer.

It is very important as a Christian that you do not allow yourself to be distracted from your daily discipline of prayer and Bible reading. The fundamentals of prayer and Bible reading and the ability to apply those principles to complex daily activities allow God to use you for bigger responsibilities in his kingdom. If you allow yourself to get distracted, then you will drift away from God's plan, and his plan is always better than anything you and I can create.

Pete discovered God's plan for his life. He grew in his love for Christ and learned how to be obedient to God. As he learned, he kept his hand on the plow and sowed many seeds for God's kingdom that fell on fertile soil.

Prayer: Dear Father God, may I grow in my love for you and be obedient daily so that I can be about doing the work you have planned for me. In Jesus's name. Amen.

BK28
WHAT IS WORTH ETERNAL LIFE?

Ecclesiastes 2:11

> Yet when I surveyed all that my hands have made, and
> what I have toiled to achieve, everything is meaningless;
> a chasing after the wind, nothing is gained under the sun.

Solomon penned this very poignant verse in Ecclesiastes 2:11:
"No matter what my hands have made, and what I have toiled to
achieve, everything is meaningless; a chasing after the wind, nothing is gained under the sun."

Thirty-five-year-old Pete Maravich was a millionaire, a
successful gardener, investor, husband, father, and had been one
of the great basketball players of all time. But he was miserable.
When I break down the verse from Ecclesiastes 2:11, it sums up
Pete's life.

"Yet when I surveyed all that my hands have made." Pete was
perhaps the greatest ball handler and had one of the best pair of
hands in the history of basketball. His legendary tricks and passes
have thrilled fans everywhere.

"And what I have toiled to achieve." Pete once told legendary
coach Red Auerbach, "You don't get this good by wishing." Pete
spent thousands of sweat equity hours perfecting his ball-handling
skills to become a great player.

"Everything is meaningless." Pete enjoyed immense fame and fortune that few people will ever achieve, but the whole experience left him empty. His life had no purpose.

"A chasing after the wind." Pete once drove his Porsche 130 miles per hour along the banks of Lake Pontchartrain in Louisiana and thought about turning his steering wheel ten degrees to the right, driving into the lake, and ending it all because he was so miserable. Pete had set fifty or sixty scoring records, but none of them made his team a champion.

"Nothing is gained under the sun." Pete never achieved the most important goal that his dad told him would make him a winner. That goal was the world championship ring. Pete bitterly left the Celtics in training camp during the season that Boston won the title in 1981.

But there was a joyous ending to Pete's story. In desperation one evening, Pete knelt by the side of his bed at five thirty in the morning and received Christ. The Holy Spirit came into Pete's heart, and Pete lived a full life for Christ during the last five years of his life.

Pete used his hands again to make the Pistol Pete Homework Basketball videos that millions have enjoyed since 1987. Pete toiled twelve-hour days to make the videos in the summer in a hot Louisiana gymnasium. This endeavor had meaning because Pete passed along his basketball artistry less than six months before he died in a gym in Pasadena, California. Pete stopped chasing the wind and seeking worldly pleasure under the sun and instead found the joy that he had missed for the first thirty-five years of his life.

Prayer: Father God, you certainly work in mysterious and creative ways. Thank you for what can be learned from the wonderful legacy of Pistol Pete. In Jesus's holy name. Amen.

BK29
AND ONE!

Romans 8:26

The Holy Spirit prays for us with such feeling that it cannot be described in words. (TLB)

The saying "And one!" is very popular among basketball fans. Every fan thrills to see the old-fashioned three-point play when a flashy guard takes the ball to the basket, gets hit as he goes up, and twists his body to spin the ball off the glass into the basket. The fans leap to their feet, high-five each other, and scream, "And one!"

"And one" means that the basket counts, and the player receives a free throw to convert the three-point play. In addition to the two-point basket, the player receives a bonus as a reward for the excellent play.

When you confess to God for the first time that you truly desire to turn away from your sinful life, God will grant you forgiveness because Jesus paid the penalty for your sin when he died on the cross. When you then place your trust in Jesus as your Savior, you receive God's free gift of grace and eternal life in heaven. You also receive an "and one" bonus because the same Holy Spirit that descended upon Jesus like a dove, and the same Holy Spirit that Jesus promised the disciples as a Comforter and Helper, takes up residence inside you as a person.

Hard to understand? Don't try to figure it out; just trust it. From the moment you receive Christ, the Holy Spirit takes up residence inside you to help with your daily problems. Concerned because you don't know how to pray or what to pray for? The Holy Spirit fills the gaps with such passion that I can't describe it here. In fact, it can't be described anywhere. It's so awesome. Remember repentance, forgiveness, and eternal life in heaven is through trust in Jesus Christ. And One, the Holy Spirit, will be with you forever.

Prayer: Father God, you are so good to me. Thank you for your blessings each day, and thank you for sending the Holy Spirit to live inside of me and guide me for the rest of my days. In Jesus's name. Amen.

BK30
DO YOU KNOW JESUS, OR DO YOU
THINK YOU KNOW JESUS?

Matthew 7:23

I never knew you.

Ralph Sampson was a seven-feet-four-inches-tall basketball star and three-time collegiate All-American at the University of Virginia from 1980–1983 and played in the NBA for the Houston Rockets. He could dribble the ball behind his back and run the fast break like a guard, a truly astounding talent.

I heard this story about him from a former referee, who was an instructor at a basketball referee camp that I attended one summer at Robert Morris College in Pittsburgh. The storyteller was Dan Wooldridge, a long-time Atlantic Coast Conference referee. One night in Charlottesville, Dan made a questionable foul call against Ralph. The UVA fans went ballistic, which they tend to do when you assess a phantom foul against the most important player in a big ACC game. Ralph raised both arms high in the air, assuring his fans that he didn't touch his opponent. Wooldridge walked into the lane, looked up at Ralph, and said, "Ralph, I think you got him on the elbow," tapping his elbow to signify where he thought the contact happened. Ralph frowned and said, "Mr. Wooldridge, don't think it's a foul. Know it's a foul!" In other words, *know* that you have a foul before you call one.

Several years ago, Ralph was at Lassiter High School to watch his son play basketball. I introduced myself, recounted the story, and asked him if it was true. He nodded and said that was pretty much what had happened. He quickly added that Dan Wooldridge was a good guy.

Do you *know* that you are going to heaven, or do you think you are going? There is as big a difference between thinking and knowing as there is between black and white. If you think you know Jesus, you probably don't. For years, I occasionally wondered if my good works with the church basketball program would get me into heaven. But the night I heard Pete Maravich tell how Christ had transformed him, I could see it clearly. Pete quoted Jesus from Matthew 7:23, "I never knew *you*. Depart from me you who practice lawlessness." I knew that Jesus knew Pete, and I *knew* that Christ did *not know* me. I desperately vowed in my heart that I wanted my life to change, and it was at that moment that Jesus Christ knew me.

I never knew you. Because they came from Jesus, those are four of the saddest words in the Bible. I pray that you will come face to face with the realization that Christ either knows you or doesn't and that you know that your name is in the Book of Life or it isn't. If you aren't sure, remove any doubt by turning from your sinful ways and inviting Christ to come into your life.

Prayer: Father God, thank you for your divine Word that teaches me what I need to do to go to heaven when I die. Lead me, Holy Spirit, so that I will confess my sins and that Jesus will know me. In Jesus's name. Amen.

BK31
MASTER THE FUNDAMENTALS

Exodus 20:1–17, Joshua 1:8, Galatians 3:24

Wherefore the Law was our schoolmaster to bring us unto Christ ...

Galatians 3:24 (KJV)

Pete Maravich was arguably the greatest ball handler, dribbler, and passer the game has ever seen. Pete's repertoire of trick passes, fancy dribbles, and ball-handling drills are unparalleled even today. The Pistol put fans on the edge of their seats when he would cross half-court on a three-on-two fast break because they might see a pass they had never seen. Once an official called a travel on Pete for a slap pass, where Pete waves his hand over the ball and slaps it to a teammate. Pete questioned him, "How can you call that? You've never seen that move." But Pete learned those amazing moves by building up to them.

When he was a kid, his father and coach, Press Maravich, taught him the fundamentals of dribbling and passing. Dribble with the right hand, now with the left, alternate left and right. Execute the bounce pass, the chest bounce pass, and the baseball pass. Later came between-the-legs, behind-the-back, around-the-neck, and over-the-shoulder passes. Once Pete mastered the basics, he moved onto the advanced skills.

In a similar fashion, a person needs to master the fundamentals of the law in the form of the Ten Commandments. Every person is a born sinner, but first, one must learn the Ten Commandments to recognize sin. When you commit a sin and know that you broke one or more of the rules, you will realize that you need to repent and ask for God's forgiveness.

Too many people essentially want to throw the behind-the-back pass without learning the chest pass. They want the saving grace of the gospel before executing the fundamental of repentance. When they don't lead with repentance, they wonder years later why God failed them.

"Well, I gave my heart to Christ that night. Why am I still doing the same old same old?" First comes knowledge of the law and the realization of sinfulness that violates that law. Then comes a verdict of the lawlessness by the Holy Spirit, leading to godly sorrow, repentance, and then salvation through the cleansing blood of the Lamb.

Remember repentance first, then place your trust in Christ. Repentance won't save you, but you can't be saved without it. Who said it? Peter Press Maravich said it several years after accepting Christ as his Savior and Lord.

Prayer: Father God, I get confused sometimes and wonder what comes first. Help me always to know and share that repentance comes before accepting Christ. In the name of Jesus, who shed his blood at Calvary to cover my sins, amen.

BK32
CEDAR GROVE GYM

Galatians 3:24, 1 John 1:7

If we walk in the Light as He is in the Light, we have fellowship with one another, and the blood of Jesus Christ cleanses us from all sin.

1 John 1:7

Dad was ninety-five years old when my brother L.E. and I convinced him to ride fifteen miles to Cedar Grove one Sunday morning after church to see the gym where he coached his state championship team in 1951. Dad had his best basketball teams in the 1950s in that gym. The Cedar Grove community had preserved the exterior with tin siding, but the gym had been locked and boarded up for years. I desperately wanted to see inside the gym one more time. It had been the early 1970s since I had been inside when it was used as a community skating rink. As a teenager, I didn't appreciate the memories, not all of which were pleasant. When I was four, I fell down the bleachers and busted my mouth. I remember Mom holding a cup full of ice to my face before she had to keep score of the basketball game for Dad.

I walked behind the hallowed gym amid broken glass, weeds, and underbrush. I saw a three-foot square opening in the back wall about twelve feet above the ground because a fan had been removed. I managed to climb up rusty scaffolding and on my tiptoes I could see inside.

There it was. I can't describe the thrill to look inside and see the court. The backboards were gone, but the solid oak planks in the floor were still in good shape. I could faintly make out the baseline. Folding chairs were scattered about the far end of the gym. Most of the bleachers were still in place on the left side.

The reason that I could see at all was because there was a hole in the tin roof on the left side. The sunlight peered through the opening and lit the gym floor like a spotlight. Dust particles danced in the sunbeam as if part of a stream. What a thrill that I will always remember.

When God shines his Light upon us, it enables us to see our flaws in spite of our darkness. We can see the sin that we need to confess to God. Without the Light, we would continue to live in darkness. We need the contrast of good to highlight the evil. Without God's rules to correct us, we have no hope of shining his Light for the world to see how a Christian is supposed to live. We need the bright Light to reveal all of the sinful crevices in our hearts that can only be cleansed with the powerful cleansing blood of Jesus Christ.

I had wanted to see the inside of that gym for many years. When I finally saw it, it wasn't exactly what I expected. But it was such a thrill to rekindle fond memories that it felt like a little slice of heaven. Surely our reward will be so much greater when we see Jesus, the True Light, face-to-face one day.

Prayer: Thank you, Father God, for the special moments when I feel your presence and get a sense of what it will be like one day to come face to face in your holy presence. Until that time, may I live under the Light and allow the Light to show me where I need to be cleansed. In Jesus's holy name. Amen.

BK33
RULEBOOK OFFICIAL

I officiated college basketball for fifteen years and called about four hundred games at various levels, including a handful of Division I games. But first I refereed high school games. Each year, I had to pass a rules test or attend a rules clinic to certify that I understood the rules of basketball. Not only did I need to know the rules, but I needed to know how to interpret the spirit and intent of the rules. Once I understood the intent of the rules, I had to be able to apply the interpretation successfully. To be a successful college official, I had to apply the rules according to the level of play. There are certain calls in college that will put you back into high school officiating quicker than you can say, "The principle of verticality."

It is not enough to know the rules. Some officials make 100 on the rules test each year but can't referee their way out of a wet paper bag. They don't understand the application of the rule at the level of basketball that they are officiating. These officials are known in the trade as "rule book officials," who call every ticky-tacky foul that happens and ruin the flow of the game. The most successful officials know the rules, interpret them correctly, and apply them to achieve a fairly called, consistently officiated game.

The Bible and God's law require us to know the rules (e.g., Ten Commandments), to be able to interpret the rules, *and* to apply them to our daily lives. Those persons who are able to follow the rules consistently, who love and obey God, and who know Jesus Christ will eventually achieve real success. Not success as the world defines it in terms of money, power, and fame but blessings such as joy, peace, and riches that are far beyond monetary gain. What would some famous athletes and entertainers give for peace at this point in their lives?

If we aren't careful, we can be like the rulebook official. If we become so legalistic in our interpretation of the Bible but fail to live out its principles of love, mercy, grace, and forgiveness, we miss the forest for the trees. When Saul was a member of the Pharisee sect, he tried to keep from breaking over six hundred rules each day. He even wore a box that contained the rules on his sleeve to remind him. The end result was that he had plenty of head knowledge but didn't have any heart knowledge until his encounter with Christ on the road to Damascus. This heart knowledge is the ability to apply the teachings and produce the fruit of the Spirit, which enriches the lives of others in the name of Jesus Christ.

Prayer: Father God, may I understand the rules in the Bible so that I will understand when I break them. Restore me, oh God, so that I can live in full fellowship with you and be able to apply my learning so that I can enjoy the prosperity and success that comes only from knowing you and your holy Word. In Jesus's name. Amen.

BK34
GREAT PASS!

Ephesians 5:14–20

Always give thanks for everything to our God and Father
in the name of our Lord Jesus Christ.

Ephesians 5:20 (TLB)

Coach John Wooden of UCLA was one of the great teachers of
the game of basketball. He even taught his players how to tie their
shoes and how to put on their socks properly so their feet would
not blister.

He also taught his players to thank their teammates for
good plays. When a player would make a good pass and set up a
teammate for a basket, the teammate who scored would point his
index finger at the player who made the assist, as if to say, "Great
pass!" Pointing took less energy than shouting and conveyed the
message of thanks.

Oftentimes we see a player point toward heaven or tap his
chest near his heart after a good play. Some people may think the
player is calling attention to himself. However, if the gesture is
sincere, our Father in heaven is truly receiving the glory.

When we give thanks to God, we should always do it in the
name of Jesus Christ. Jesus is ready to relay the compliment to
God on our behalf.

We should thank God when things are going great, and even when things are not going so great. Because he is the giver of all blessings, including the most precious one of all, Jesus Christ, who went to the cross for our sins.

Prayer: Father God, may I be filled with gratitude for your incomparable love, mercy, grace, and the infinite ways that you bless me. Jesus, please continue to intercede for me and give thanks for all these blessings to my most holy Maker. In Jesus's name. Amen.

BK35
IT'S AMAZING

Luke 7:44–50

You can be forgiven all your sin in half the tick of a clock,
and pass from death more swiftly than I can utter the words.

—Evangelist Charles Spurgeon

An Aerosmith song from the late 1980s has a special place in my heart. Comedian and author Wayne Federman created an awesome six-minute highlight tape of Pete Maravich's greatest plays set to this song. The lyrics fit Pete's story so well that I thought this secular song was especially written for Wayne's video until one day my friend Neal said, "Oh, that's 'Amazing' by Aerosmith."

"I put the right ones out, and took the wrong ones in." Pastor Michael McQueen reminded our St. James UMC Bible study that bad company corrupts good habits (1 Corinthians 15:33). There is a reason your family wants to know if you are hanging with the wrong crowd.

"Had an angel of mercy to see me through all my sin." Take a moment to reflect on times that God has sent an angel of mercy, an angel of protection, or a guardian angel that took you through dangerous situations. You will never really know how many times until you see the replay in heaven.

"There were times in my life when I was going insane, trying to walk through the pain." We cause ourselves pain by trying to walk through situations and decisions in life without allowing our Father to be in control. If God is in control, he can make those seemingly insane times bearable. Certainly Jesus lived through his share of insane moments with the self-righteous Pharisees, the incredibly painful walk on the pathway to Golgotha, and the hurtful desertion of the disciples during the final hours of his crucifixion.

"In the blink of an eye, you finally see the light." You can walk in darkness for many years until you finally admit it's not about you and what you can do but it's about Christ and what he did for you, how he died for your personal sin. When you admit before your Most High God that Jesus died for your sins on the cross, God will change you in the blink of an eye. You will no longer walk in spiritual darkness, and you will begin to walk in the light. It's amazing what happens when the Holy Spirit comes into you the moment you receive Christ into your cleansed self.

Are you discouraged by a family crisis? Have you been deserted by a friend? Are you struggling in school? You've got nothing to lose and everything to gain. Just let God do what he can do. Let go and let God. Pete Maravich finally let go, and I finally let go, and God changed us for eternity. He changed us, and he can change you. "In the blink of an eye, you finally see the light."

Prayer: Dear Father, thank you for the lyrics that Wayne Federman overlaid on the Maravich video. The video spoke to me, and it can speak to others. Thank you for the lyrics and videos that can help us communicate your transforming power and grace. In Jesus's name. Amen.

BK36
SEE THE FLOOR

Matthew 2:1–12

When they saw the star, they rejoiced with exceeding great joy.

Matthew 2:10

One of the most exciting plays in basketball is the fast break. The purpose of the fast break is to move the ball as quickly as possible down the floor before the defense gets back. A well-timed fast break will result in a layup, slam dunk, or three-pointer. A successful fast break energizes the crowd and fills the team with confidence and energy. My father taught his high school teams a great fast break, and several times his teams scored over a hundred points in a regulation game.

When the player in the middle of the break dribbles with his head up, he can see all of the passing and driving options in front of him. Even better is to have a player with excellent peripheral vision to see players with a 180-degree vision. People thought that Pete Maravich must have had eyes in the back of his head the way that he passed the ball to teammates who were trailing him on the break. It's important for young players to learn to dribble with their heads up so that they can see the floor. When your head is down, you can't see where you are going, and you won't see the players who are open on the wing or breaking to the basket.

The three wise men who came from the east had their heads up to see and follow the star. They kept looking up to follow the star until it stopped above the manger. The wise men paid attention to God's calling and the clues about Jesus's birth. They were very brave because they could have been killed by Julius Caesar for finding Jesus and not killing him.

It's important to look to God each day for guidance in living as a Christian. By keeping our heads up spiritually, we can be ready to make the right plays as we live out each day for him. When we allow the world's cares to make us drop our heads in sadness, despair, or frustration, we miss the people to whom God would have us witness and we miss the blessings that God places in our paths. We need the power of God to keep our heads up and eyes alert for chances to serve the kingdom.

Prayer: Father God, thank you for the wise men who followed the star. Help me keep my head up when tough times happen so that I can still see the plays that you would have me make for your kingdom. In Jesus's name. Amen.

BK37
IT'S A SLOW FADE

1 John 3:4

For sin is the transgression of the Law. (KJV)

I shared a random story at open gym about a highly touted high school prospect from Durham, North Carolina, named John Wall. John was rated the number-one point guard nationally. Apparently, John and his friends entered a vacant home without permission. Fortunately, no one was harmed. John received a misdemeanor and began his college career as planned.

I told the boys that it is important to walk with Christ each day because the further you get separated from God, the worse your choices are likely to be. The worse your choices are the worse your consequences will be. The teenagers had no business being in that house. One choice can lead to another choice and then another until one day you find yourself in the wrong place at the wrong time. Casting Crowns offered a stirring song called "Slow Fade" that I played for the boys. "It's a slow fade, when you give yourself away… People never crumble in a day." I shared with the boys that I wanted them to be really careful over the summer and not do stupid stuff. You usually don't just do something really stupid unless you've done some less stupid stuff and gotten away with it. "Thoughts invade, choices made, a price will be paid when you give yourself away…" It can happen to anyone when he or she lets his or her guard down.

John Wall was very fortunate. He could have been shot for being an intruder. His rise to fame made the story much more memorable. Wall signed with the University of Kentucky, arguably the most storied program in the history of college basketball. Immediately, he triggered a wave of enthusiasm and optimism in the Big Blue Nation that had not been seen since the 1997–1998 season. A few overzealous Kentucky fans called him Blue Jesus, a takeoff on former New York Knicks star Earl "The Pearl" Monroe's playground nickname of Black Jesus. Wall's explosive speed to the basket with the ball is unparalleled, and he was the number one pick in the 2010 NBA draft. He led the Wildcats to an SEC championship, an Elite Eight appearance, and a 35-3 record. During the season, Wall endeared himself to UK fans by handling himself with poise, humility, and teamwork and played extremely hard at both ends of the floor. During the first semester, John had the highest GPA on the team and made the Freshman Academic All-SEC team during second semester. But it could have all been for naught if the circumstances in that house had been different.

Prayer: Lord, thank you for the mercy that you have shown me many times when I've done stupid stuff and I didn't receive what I deserved. I thank you for your patience with me and your guiding hand that gives me a chance to convert for you. In Jesus's name. Amen.

BK38
BEWARE OF TECHNICAL FOULS

John 14:26, Romans 8:26, Ephesians 4:29

Don't use bad language. Say only what is helpful and good to those you are talking to, and what will give them a blessing.

Ephesians 4:29 (TLB)

My father and father-in-law were both high school basketball coaches and principals. My dad, Coach Lester Farr, coached over 1,200 ball games and received only three technical fouls. That's one per decade, which is pretty doggone amazing. Once, he was convinced that the officials were calling too many fouls on his team. Dad called a time-out and told his player in the huddle loud enough for the official to hear, "Virginia, when that girl comes near you, I want you to run up in the stands so that you can't foul her." Whistle, T!

My father-in-law, Damon Ray, also helped the officials from time to time when he was the principal at East Hardin High School in Kentucky. Ray enjoyed roaming the far sideline while the game was in progress to keep an eye on the officials. One official said to him, "Are there twelve of you? You're over here under the basket, you're over there, and then you're under the other basket." Another official came over and tried to put his lanyard and whistle around Ray's neck, indicating, "You're going to help us anyway." When he passed away in 2008, the funeral services were appropriately held in that gymnasium to accommodate the crowd.

A technical foul should be called when an official feels that a player or coach has exceeded the proper decorum via unsportsmanlike conduct such as swearing or arguing too much. A certain amount of tension is expected in hard-fought games, and a well-timed technical foul can diffuse a volatile situation and keep the game under control.

Our conscience combined with the Holy Spirit lets us know immediately when we have overstepped our bounds through anger and improper speech. The moment we snap at someone or are rude to someone, no matter how irritating the person was, our conscience/Holy Spirit calls a T on us. If it's bad enough, I get that sinking feeling in my stomach and yucky taste in my mouth, and that's the technical foul. It's time for an immediate apology when that situation occurs. Then you're freed up to stay connected with God, or else you'll be riding the pine until you come clean.

Prayer: Most wonderful Father God, thank you for my conscience and the Holy Spirit that whistles those actions that I wish I could take back. Help me have the courage to follow through and apologize when I should and as I should. In Jesus's name. Amen.

BK39
SOMETIMES YOU GOTTA CUT
SOME FOLKS LOOSE!

Proverbs 13:20

He that walks with wise men shall be wise, but the
companion of fools shall be destroyed.

I was a starting guard on my high school basketball team as a
fifteen-year-old junior at five feet six inches tall and 115 pounds.
What a physical specimen. Our new coach, Coach Bowman, put
our team through the most grueling conditioning program that
any of us had ever experienced. The dividends certainly did not
pay off during the first half of the season. In fact, we were 2-9
going into our road game at Adrian High School. At halftime
that night, we were down by thirty-one, 62-31, when we hit rock
bottom. Our two leading rebounders were giggling when Coach
Bowman was talking, and the next thing we knew, they had quit
the squad. To say we were discouraged when we left the gym that
night would be an understatement.

However, things turned for the better. Coach Bowman
revamped our offense and went with three guards to give us more
quickness. Our superior conditioning paid off in the second half of
games. We reeled off seven wins in our next ten games, including
a stunning upset of the state's number-two-ranked team in our

classification. There is no question that our team rallied and united to salvage the season after those two players left the team.

Sometimes it is necessary for us to disassociate ourselves from some folks who are dragging us into their sinful lifestyles. We're no better or worse than these folks. As Christians, we are supposed to associate with unbelievers because they need what we have, which is a relationship with Jesus Christ. Jesus said that he came to heal the sick, and he was certainly comfortable in the presence of sinners. However, Jesus never caved into their sinful desires. The line that we are not to cross is when we start committing the same sins as our friends. If we sense that they are dragging us into bad habits, it's time to hang with another crowd.

Paul focused solely on Christ when he preached to the Corinthians about their sinful lifestyles, but Paul never adopted their lurid habits. We get into trouble when we start to imitate lifestyles that are not of Christ. There is only one lifestyle that should be emulated, and that lifestyle is the sinless one exhibited by Jesus Christ. To follow the lifestyle of Christ, we might need to let some folks go who are dragging us through the mud. Sometimes we've just gotta cut some folks loose.

Prayer: Dear Father God, please help me realize right away when I'm being dragged into sinful living by others. Give me the godly confidence that I can hang with them and try to influence them for Christ without slipping myself. In Jesus's name. Amen.

BK40
PULLING ON THE DOG'S EARS

Proverbs 21:9, 26:17

You get a mad dog by the ears when you butt into a quarrel
that's not of your business.

Proverbs 26:17 (MSG)

My wonderful wife, Becca, is a fervent University of Kentucky
basketball fan. She converted me and our girls, Allison and Jillian,
to cheer for the Cats when the girls were very young. After all, it's
pretty easy to cheer for the winningest college basketball program
of all time. The knowledge, dedication, and passion of the UK
fans is second to none, and Becca is no exception.

I bought two center-court seats for a UK-Georgia game in
Athens, and we were the only people for Kentucky in that section.
Early in the game, she clacked her clacker shaker at a Georgia
free throw shooter. *Hmm. She's a little more fired up than usual,*
I observed. Midway through the first half, Georgia's seven-foot,
275-pound power forward gave UK's 180-pound point guard a
shove from behind on a drive to the basket on a fast break. The UK
player flew through the air like Superman and landed on his chin
at the feet of the Georgia cheerleaders. He lay motionless on the
floor and left the game with a concussion. Becca was infuriated.
She leaped out of her seat in a flash and yelled at the official, "Call
an intentional foul! That was intentional! C'mon!"

That's when the Georgia fan sitting to her right made his first mistake. He commented loudly and condescendingly, "*That* wasn't intentional."

Becca whirled around and said, "Bull! He shoved him on purpose!"

Trying to diffuse the situation, I told the guy, "Look, she thinks she just lost her point guard for the season. Just let it go."

Ten seconds later, I heard, "Don't you touch me!" He placed his hand on her shoulder to tell her something else, and that was his second mistake. If you are a stranger, you don't touch my wonderful wife when she is emotional about her Wildcats!

I had always wanted to meet former Bulldog Herb White because Herb played against Pete Maravich at LSU and with Pete on the Atlanta Hawks. Herb was sitting below us, but I thought, *That can wait until another day.*

Do you realize that the Bible addresses this type of situation? I never realized it until I read Proverbs 26:17 one day. This gentleman had no business touching Becca, and he didn't have any business commenting on the disagreement between Becca and the referee. The Bible makes it clear in the book of Proverbs that intervening in an argument between two people is as foolish as pulling on a dog's ears. Many people read one Proverbs chapter a day, 31 chapters in a month, for knowledge, wisdom, and discernment. Study Proverbs to expand your knowledge for daily living and stay out of trouble.

Prayer: Dear Heavenly Father, thank you so much for the wisdom that can be gleaned from studying the book of Proverbs. Help me to absorb the knowledge that will keep me in step with your intentions for my daily walk. In Jesus's name. Amen.

BK41
IT'S A LONG SEASON

Psalm 119:105, John 14:26, 1 Thessalonians 5:17

Pray without ceasing.

1 Thessalonians 5:17

A top major college basketball team will play between thirty-five and forty games in a five-month season. After two-a-day practices in October, teams will usually open their season against weaker opponents in November before playing tougher games in December. The team plays its conference season in January and February when the really tough games occur. Then comes the conference tournament in March, and if the team has performed well enough, the reward of March Madness awaits. The best teams will reach the pinnacle of the Final Four on the first full weekend in April, and one team will be crowned NCAA champion for the season. Next comes personal training and preparation over the spring and summer.

Before each game, the point guard must learn the particular defenses that the opponent will use to thwart the team's offense. The trickier the defenses the more preparation is necessary. The point guard is especially important since he or she initiates the offensive plays. If the point guard simply relied on prior knowledge and failed to practice for the next team's defense, he or she would throw the wrong pass or run the wrong offensive plays, which would create more turnovers than assists and fewer points. If the point guard commits too many turnovers, he or she will end up on the bench and possibly lose a starting position for several games or the entire season.

As a Christian, you can't rely on what you learned in Sunday school or from the sermon and expect that you will get through the week on that practice. There are games to be played every day as Satan throws different wrinkles, situations, temptations, and obstacles at you to trip you up. These obstacles are specifically designed to get you to commit sin (turnovers). That's why you must practice each day, praying with God and reading his Word, to minimize the mistakes (turnovers) and maximize the good deeds (assists) in the name of Christ.

Most medicines for illnesses and maintaining good health are taken daily. You can't take seven pills in one day and optimize your physical health all week. You need a steady dosage. It's that way with prayer and scripture. A steady daily dose of prayer and scripture will keep your spiritual health in good order. Refuse to take any days off with God, and you'll see your assist-to-turnover (good deed to sin) ratio improve dramatically. With the Holy Spirit living in you and Jesus living in your heart, you've got plenty of help to make the right plays for God. You'll get through the long season in flying colors for the kingdom.

Prayer: Father God, thank you that I get the chance to practice daily by praying and reading your Word. Help me be consistent so that I'm always ready for the trick defenses that Satan throws my way. May I always honor you in all that I do. In Jesus's name. Amen.

BK42
KAY YOW (1942–2009)

Romans 8:18

Yet what we suffer now is nothing compared to the glory
that we will receive later. (TLB)

For more than thirty years, women's basketball coaches sought
guidance from Kay Yow, the head women's basketball coach at
North Carolina State University. An undeniable legend in the
sport, her bio reads like an excerpt from College Basketball's Most
Desirable Accomplishments. But when thumbing through the
pages of that biography, you'll discover that Yow's fiercest competitor wasn't on the court.

Four times, Yow was diagnosed with breast cancer, most
recently stage IV in 2008. But like any other rival, she showed
up for cancer's game, determined to fight. In an interview with
Sharing the Victory, the magazine of the Fellowship of Christian
Athletes, Kay explained her faith and the source of her strength to
fight cancer on four different occasions.

STV: Have you ever wondered why cancer happened to
       you?

KY: I've never questioned why I have cancer. I have an
       idea, but I know that God has a plan for me, and I
       just try to trust his plan and what it is that he wants

me to do. That is the main thing. I do know that he loves me and that it is a love that is deep. I know he wants the best for me. I feel sort of fortunate to even get a little bit of an answer. I wouldn't expect one, but I don't want to miss what he wants me to get out of all of this.

Prayer: Father God, thank you for the inspiring legacy of Kay Yow. May I learn from the trust and faith that she placed in you that I can overcome the obstacles in my life by relying on you to be my strength. In the holy name of Jesus. Amen.

BK43
"PISTOL PETE" MARAVICH
(1947–1988)

Ecclesiastes 2:11

> Yet when I surveyed all that my hands have made, and what
> I have toiled to achieve, everything was meaningless. A
> chasing after the wind, nothing was gained under the sun.

Pete Maravich is recognized as one of the legends in the game
of basketball. "Pistol Pete," who got his nickname from a sportswriter because he shot from the hip in the eighth grade, became
the all-time leading scorer ever in college basketball. His popularity reached an all-time high for a college basketball player during
his three-year career at Louisiana State University. He averaged
just over 44 points a game when freshmen could not play on the
varsity, and there was no three-point line!

Despite his success on the court, Pete was miserable off the
court. He shared some of the many things he tried to satisfy
his soul. At the depth of his despair, Maravich remembered the
message of hope that he heard at a Campus Crusade for Christ
event in San Bernardino, California in 1966, just before entering
LSU.

"At the height of my popularity, I was miserable. I plunged
into karate, Hinduism, reincarnation, TM, and UFOs. I became

a radical nutritionist and a vegetarian. I took life-extending drugs from Eastern Europe …Then I began thinking, 'Why am I here? Is this all there is to life?' I had rejected Christ at nineteen and gone back into the wilderness, and I hated it.

"In 1980, I quit basketball out of pride and immaturity. I was so bitter I divorced myself from everything in basketball. I stayed home, changed my phone numbers, and moped for two years. Then one fateful night in November 1982, I could not sleep. All the sins of my youth kept parading through my mind all night. I cried out to God, suddenly remembering the gist of the prayer offered at that Campus Crusade for Christ sixteen years earlier. I asked Jesus to come into my life. Nothing gave me the peace that Jesus gave me that night."

Pete was transformed that evening and dedicated his life to sharing Jesus Christ with as many people as possible through speaking engagements and his basketball camp in Clearwater, Florida. In 1988 he died tragically on a basketball court at the Church of the Nazarene in Pasadena, California, while playing the game he loved with Dr. James Dobson and his friends.

Prayer: Father God, thank you for the lessons that I can learn from Pete's life. No matter how much fame and success that I have as measured by the world's standards, only Jesus Christ can ever satisfy the longing that I have within my soul. In Jesus's name. Amen.

BK44
DAVID ROBINSON

Matthew 5:14

You are the light of the world. A city that is set on a hill cannot be hidden.

If David Robinson had not been a late bloomer, he would have never entered the US Naval Academy. The academy will not allow anyone over six feet six inches tall to enter Annapolis. That was David's height as a freshman, but he quickly grew five more inches! Nicknamed "The Admiral" while he was at Navy, Robinson became the most celebrated basketball player ever at Navy and enjoyed a stellar career as an Olympian and NBA World Champion with the San Antonio Spurs. David shares his story of receiving his "second birth" when he committed his life to Jesus Christ.

David Robinson has been called the Goliath of giving. For at least ten years beginning in the mid-nineties, Robinson has given ten percent of his substantial income to the David Robinson Foundation and has physically given his time and energy. Matthew 5:14 sets the tone and defines the work of his foundation. Robinson said, "God has given me more than I ever hoped for, so it's my responsibility to give back."

In an interview with Eads Home Ministries, David recalled the circumstances of his second birthday, which was the day that he received Christ as his Savior on June 8, 1991. David explained,

"That day, Christ became a real person to me … I felt like a spoiled brat. Everything was about me, me, me. How much money can I make? It was all about David's praise and David's glory. I had never stopped to honor God for all he had done for me. That really hit me. I cried all afternoon. That very day, I was saved."

Prayer: Father God, thank you for David Robinson and the legacy of his foundation in San Antonio that has helped thousands of young people enjoy a better life. May I learn from David's generous giving of both time and money to honor you with gifts of my own. In the name of Jesus. Amen.

BK45
DO YOU WARRANT A
SPECIAL DEFENSE?

Psalm 21:11–13, Ephesians 6:10–18

Be strong in the Lord, and in His great power!

Ephesians 6:10

Suppose that you play on a NCAA Division I basketball team. If you are one of the weakest players and your grade point average is higher than your minutes per game or scoring average, you are surely a bench warmer who rarely gets into the game. The opposing team doesn't do any special preparation to stop you since you don't score points. You probably aren't a threat to them defensively either.

But pretend that you are the leading scorer on your team. In fact, you lead the conference in scoring at thirty points per game and ten assists per game. You are a bona fide, prime time superstar. The opposing teams plot late into the night to slow you down and take you out of your game. The opponents will try trick defenses, double teams, and aggressive defenders. The opposing coach will do anything that he can to make you less productive.

Take an unbeliever, a person who does not know Jesus Christ and has not accepted Christ as Savior or a lukewarm Christian who has stopped working for the Lord because of some stronghold that has separated the person from God. Folks who are separated from God are of no threat to Satan. These people have the same abilities and talents as believers do, but they aren't wired to God.

But if you are a believer with a passion for reaching the lost, you had better know that Satan is burning the midnight oil trying to shut you down. Satan is probing every nook and cranny to find the chinks in your armor. It could be lust, or a sports team, or a sport, or money, or positional power, or selfishness that Satan uses to take you out of your game.

Satan doesn't follow the rules and will use any scheme possible to deceive you. The devil will throw up distractions, obstacles, doubts, half-truths, diversions, and selfish desires to derail you. If Satan can derail a pastor or a believer, it could mean hundreds of people will not come to know Christ.

You need God's incomparably mighty power and protection from Satan's schemes more than ever before. Be wary that Satan is out there, waiting to thwart you, just like the teams that go up against the superstars. Know that daily you need God's special power through his Word and frequent prayer to continue to shine his light.

Prayer: Father God, thank you so much for the tools you give me to ward off the evil clutches and ways of the devil. You are so much stronger, and the devil knows it, and I know it. Flee from me, Satan, because I have God's mighty power through Jesus and the Holy Spirit. In Jesus's name. Amen.

BK46
GOT ENOUGH POINTS?

Ephesians 2:9

Not because of works, lest any man should boast.

"Pistol Pete" Maravich was one of the all-time greatest basketball players and is recognized as the most innovative player because he changed the face of basketball with his spectacular Showtime array of passing and dribbling wizardry. Pete became a tremendous evangelist for Christ after his playing days ended and traveled the country and the globe proclaiming the good news through his powerful testimony. God still uses Pete because when the latest hotshot guard comes along, there is a leap back in time to compare the latest phenom to Pistol. That's one way the legend of Pete Maravich is remembered. There are several hundred videos of Pete Maravich on YouTube so young people can marvel at his tremendous skills and hear his testimonies.

Pete shared this story in one of his testimonies to illustrate that you cannot earn your way to heaven no matter what title you hold or how great your accomplishments are. Only by the grace of God are we saved.

A senior pastor approached the pearly gates and was greeted by St. Peter, who told him that he needed a hundred points to get into heaven. The pastor proclaimed that he had been the senior pastor at a five-thousand-member church.

"One point," St. Peter replied.

Somewhat perplexed, the pastor said, "Well, I started four orphanages."

"Two points," came the reply.

"I served dinner to fifteen thousand homeless people every Thanksgiving."

"Three points. What about Jesus? Do you know Jesus?" asked St. Peter.

The pastor said, "Yes, I know Jesus Christ."

"That's worth a hundred points. Come on in," St. Peter said as he welcomed the pastor to heaven.

Certainly "faith without works is dead" (James 2:17). As Christians, we are recognized by the fruit that we bear once we are saved, but good works alone will never get us into heaven. First and foremost, we must know Christ to enter the gates of heaven. How many points do you have?

Prayer: Father God, thank you for your free gift of saving grace that cost Jesus his life. I am so thankful that I don't have to earn my way into heaven because I could never perform enough good works. But I appreciate the opportunity to show people through my works that Christ lives in me. In Jesus's name. Amen.

BK47
YOU CAN GO 1-0!

Psalm 118:24, Matthew 6:25–33, Colossians 3:17

This is the day that the Lord has made, let us rejoice and be glad in it.

Psalm 118:24 (KJV)

I want to sign Your Name to the end of this day.

—*Lifesong* by Casting Crowns

Kentucky basketball is back thanks to coach John Calipari, who brought in a slew of hotshot freshmen for the 2009–2010 season and brought back a swagger that the Cats had been missing. In January UK was 16-0 and ranked second in the country. Coach Cal was the first to admit that there were several games that UK could have lost but for the heroics of super frosh John Wall. On the day before UK played undermanned Hartford, Cal was asked about UK's next game after Hartford against bitter rival Louisville. Cal insisted that he had watched no tape of Louisville and would not until after the Hartford game. Calipari's approach is to take it one game at a time no matter who the next opponent is and focus intently on the immediate game. By focusing on only one game, he relieves pressure on the team from rabid fans who believe he can win 'em all.

I received an e-mail from Rick Johnson, the head coach of the Trinity Lady Crusaders (Dublin, Georgia), who were also unbeaten midway through the 2009–2010 season with a perfect 17-0 record. Coach Johnson acknowledged that the winning streak was exciting, but he said that he controlled the pressure by trying to go 1-0. Each game is a mini-season. You start 0-0. If you win the game, you're 1-0. Then you go back to 0-0 and get ready for the next one.

You and I can choose to go 1-0 or 0-1. God gives us one day at a time, and each day, we decide how we will spend it. We can worry and ignore God and try to do it all ourselves or we can rejoice in the day he gives us and live it for him. Start each morning in the Word and talk to God. This pre-game preparation before we come out of the tunnel (go through the front door) gives us a great chance to live that day for God. With God by our side throughout the day, we've got a great shot at going 1-0 by putting up a W for God and hanging an L on the biggest loser of all time. You could go 0-1 by compartmentalizing God and intentionally not allowing him to come to work or school with you. "Hey, God," and, "Good night, God," with nothing in the middle won't cut it. He is interested in everything we do and yearns to help us if we will only look to him.

Can we possibly go 30-0 for God? It seems impossible, so take it one day at a time and go 1-0 again and again. Going 1-0 doesn't mean without sin, but it does mean obedience. God always gives us sufficient strength for today. Today has plenty of challenges without worrying about tomorrow. Today I had a 1-0 mind-set, and it paid positive dividends. I've got a shot at putting together a win streak come tomorrow.

Prayer: Most wonderful and mighty God, help me go 1-0 today as a person, as a friend, as a servant, as a brother or sister in Christ, as a disciple. When my head hits the pillow tonight, I want to know that I put this day in the win column for you. In the name of the One who took my place. Amen.

BK48
HOW WILLING ARE YOU
TO STAND UP FOR ME?

Matthew 10:32–33

Whosoever therefore shall confess me before men, him will I confess also before My Father which is in heaven.

Matthew 10:32

During a testimony in Shreveport, Louisiana, Pete Maravich once shared this story, which he heard from a man who had been an interpreter at a Billy Graham crusade in Tokyo, Japan. The story, which is one of courage in the face of death, occurred during the sieges by Communist North Korea to stamp out Christianity, which is booming in South Korea today, perhaps because of many stories like this one.

"There were these Northern Koreans, about two hundred of them, who rounded up all the Christians in this little town (in South Korea). They made them all go inside their little church at the end of town, and the Northern Koreans said, 'All right. We're going to line you up single file. You're going to walk by this picture of Jesus Christ (which they had nailed to the inside of the front door), and you're going to spit in your Messiah's face. If you don't, you'll be shot in the head.' The first person was a man, and he walked by and spit in Jesus's face. The second man walked by and spit in his face. The third man walked by and spit in his face, as did the fourth. The next person in line was a little girl. She walked up to the picture of Christ, took her dress, and wiped the spit away. Then she said, 'Jesus, I love you, and I am willing to die for you.'"

This act of courage completely flabbergasted the Northern Koreans, and they yelled, "Get out! Everybody get out!" Later, they said that the reason they let everybody go was that to be a good Communist, you would need the undeniably strong faith of that young Christian girl. Then they took the four men who spit in Christ's face and shot them dead.

Prayer: Most holy and powerful God, I will likely never face a situation quite like the one that young girl faced, but I might face opportunities to deny you to the world. May I have just a portion of that young Korean girl's amazing courage to stand up for Jesus Christ. In Jesus's holy and precious name. Amen.

BK49
THE POWER OF THREE

John 14:16–26

And I will pray the Father, and He shall give you another Comforter, that he may abide with you forever.

John 14:16 (NIV)

I've observed over the years that any basketball team needs three reliable scorers to be a consistent winner. During the 2009–2010 season, Kentucky typically had at least three reliable scorers. However, when they played at South Carolina, there were only two, and those two could not score enough to prevent their first loss. A team needs an inside scorer, a good outside shooter, and a guard who can penetrate the lane and get off his shots. When a team is in trouble, they're going to need the three-point shooter, the inside force, or the slashing drive to the basket. That balance makes for an excellent offensive team.

John 14:16 and John 14:26 refer to all three members of the Holy Trinity: God, Jesus, and the Holy Spirit, who Jesus sometimes called the Comforter or Helper. It's very unusual to see a reference to all three in the same verse. For sure you need the help of all three to become who you need to be in Christ. First of all, God, Jesus, and the Holy Spirit existed before the beginning of time because God invented time and space when he created the world in six days and rested on the seventh. God created Adam and Eve, who lived in paradise until the fall when they were tricked by the guile of Satan. The world eventually multiplied, and generation after generation tried but failed to keep the Ten Commandments that God gave Moses on Mount Sinai for the people of Israel.

So God sent Jesus who died for our sins and rose from the grave, and Jesus sent the Holy Spirit after his ascension to heaven. God the Father, Jesus, his Son, and the Holy Spirit, the Comforter and Helper. We are Christians, believers, and children of God when we have Jesus in our hearts and have received the Holy Spirit. We need all three members of the Holy Trinity.

Jesus told his disciples, "I will be with you always, even to the end of the world." But we also received a bonus from Jesus. That bonus is the Holy Spirit, a person who dwells in us. Jesus also called the Holy Spirit the Spirit of Truth. Depending upon the situation, you can call upon the One (Jesus) when you need an intercessor, or the One (God) who loves you so much that he sent the One (Jesus) to the cross to die for our sins, or the One (Holy Spirit) who lives inside us as a person who fills in our prayer gaps and helps us with our daily problems. All three will never leave nor forsake you and will be with you always. When you receive Christ, you place yourself into eternity *now* and receive access to the three who have the power to transform the worst of sinners.

Prayer: Dear holy and precious Father, I don't really understand why there are three, but I am grateful for what each of you do in my life. I can never thank you enough, but I will try each day to count my blessings and learn to rely on you throughout all circumstances. In Jesus's holy name. Amen.

BK50
HMM...I WONDER WHAT
MY NEW NAME WILL BE

Revelation 2:12–17

And I will give him a white stone, and on the stone a new name written which no one knows except him who receives it.

Revelation 2:17

At my Friday morning Bible study group, my friend George and I swapped high school basketball stories from the glory days. Apparently, he got up the nerve to ask his coach on behalf of his teammates if the team could have their last names on the backs of their jerseys. His coach replied, "Son, if you put it in the basket enough times, they will know your name." That was the end of the discussion. Some teams are adamant about not having players' names on jerseys. Penn State football, Indiana basketball, and the New York Yankees come to mind, and those teams have three pretty good pedigrees over the years.

I have a collection of Pete Maravich throwback jerseys. All but one, the LSU jersey where Pete saw his most fame, have "Pistol" or Maravich on the back. In his seventh pro season, Pete switched from "Pistol" to Maravich after the NBA foolishly outlawed nicknames at a time that the NBA desperately needed to market its star players. By the way, Pete's senior LSU home jersey was auctioned for $103,500, a record at the time.

When I first refereed college basketball, a veteran official named Robert "Poochie" Hartsfield helped break me into the leagues. As we drove to Columbus or Savannah for games, Poochie, who worked as a pro baseball scout during the spring and summer, regaled me with stories of ACC and SEC games. Poochie once bragged, "Had [Coach Adolph] Rupp for four of his twelve home losses [at Kentucky], he ain't said a word to me yet." A Tulane coach told Poochie that he would never again referee at his gym. Poochie replied, "I've been through five Tulane coaches, and I'll be here when you're gone." The Tulane coach was fired after that season, and sure enough, Poochie sent him a letter.

My favorite Poochie anecdote happened in Baton Rouge where Pete had already reached legendary status reminiscent of another great entertainer named Elvis. Pete was on his way to one of his twenty-eight fifty-point games before a vociferous, overflow crowd at LSU's Cow Palace. But Pete's dad, LSU Coach Press Maravich, was complaining about Poochie's lack of foul calls. Press screamed, "They're killing my son in the lane! Do something about it, Poochie!" At a dead ball in front of the LSU bench, Poochie strolled nonchalantly over to Press, looked at him, and said, "Coach, I'll take care of it. (Pause) What number is he wearing?"

Poochie was making a point to Press that his son and star player would not receive preferential treatment. But Poochie knew who number 23 was, and so did everybody in the arena and in college basketball. Maravich or Pistol wasn't on the back of his jersey, but Pete put it in the basket so many times to the tune of forty-four points per game, that every basketball fan knew his name.

Our sinful human nature cries out that we want everybody to know our names. We yearn for accolades and recognition, and sometimes we forget to give God the glory. For eternity, we will either get a white stone with our new names written on it, or we won't get one. Receiving a white stone with your name on it will be better than getting the number one jersey at the NBA draft, and millions of saints and angels will applaud in heaven.

Prayer: Father God, help me play not for my name on the back of the jersey but for the Eternal Coach I represent. May all the accolades that I receive be funneled directly to you for your glory. In Jesus's name. Amen.

BK51
HE'S ALWAYS
THERE FOR YOU

1 Peter 5:7, Hebrews 13:5

Let Him have all your worries and cares, for He is always thinking about you and watching everything that concerns you.

1 Peter 5:7 (TLB)

On February 10, 2010, my family and I celebrated my dad's ninety-seventh birthday with many former students dropping by to say hello. We ate steak for lunch. Imagine yourself living to be ninety-seven and eating steak. It's a testament to Dad's determination to take good care of himself, including his teeth. As Becca and I drove down that morning, I reflected on numerous good times that we've had together. As we passed my high school, one moment stood out as I recalled how my dad was there for me when I needed help.

I was a senior at West Laurens High School in 1971–1972 during the first year that Laurens County's west side schools were consolidated. We had a pretty fair basketball team, and the excitement grew as we prepared to play Dublin High School for the first time. It was the classic "Old McDonald Had a Farm" serenade of the county school team by the Dublin students who must have thought they were some big city school in a town of fifteen thousand. We were 5-2, but Dublin was 8-0 and ranked number 2 in Class AA. An overflow crowd packed the Dublin gym, and the doors were closed thirty minutes before the girls' tipoff. We were down thirteen at the half but rallied in the second half to send the game into overtime. That's when we reeled off the first nine points in the overtime to seal the victory.

In the midst of that 9-0 run, I drew a charge against one of my best friends, who had transferred to Dublin. When Mickey fell on top of me, I caught a cramp in my right calf and screamed. As I writhed on the floor, Coach Wildes came out to see about me, and there was my dad. I don't know where he came from, but he got there as quick as a flash. I stayed in the game and made two free throws followed by an eighteen-foot jumper. My team was ecstatic as the game ended. West Laurens had upset Dublin.

I was unaware of Dad's presence during the game and didn't know where he was sitting. But I know he was thinking about me during the entire game. When I cried out and needed help, he was there in an instant. His love and concern brought him immediately out of the stands to make sure that I was all right. I have always appreciated that support when it appeared that I was injured.

Our relationship with God as believers has similarities. We are often unaware of God's presence during our trials and don't always sense his presence. But the scripture from 1 Peter 5:7 assures me that God is thinking about me and watching over me throughout the day. When I need help, God is there instantly when I reach out to him. God's love and concern for me is so infinite that he sent Jesus to the cross for me. My sin helped put Jesus there, but God's perfect love and grace kept him up there. Let's thank God every day for the unwavering love and support that comes only from God and his Son.

Prayer: Father God, thank you for my parents who were there to patch up my skinned knees, see me through disappointments, and to encourage and support me. May I return the same support for my children and their children and know that everlasting love comes from knowing Christ. Thank you for the Holy Spirit, who teaches me, leads me, and guides me. In the holy and wonderful name of our Savior, Jesus Christ. Amen.

BK52
HEAVEN'S FINAL FOUR

Jeremiah 29:11, Romans 5:8, 1 John 1:9,
John 3:16, Ephesians 2:8

But by grace you have been saved through faith…

Ephesians 2:8

In October 2009, over three hundred NCAA men's Division I teams began practice with the same dream: to make it to the Final Four on the final weekend of March Madness. The first two weeks of the 2010 tournament were filled with stunning upsets. The sixty-five-team field eventually came down to the following four teams: Butler, Michigan State, West Virginia, and Duke. These teams battled for the ultimate prize to be crowned NCAA Men's Champion for 2010. Here is how the Final Four bracket looked as the teams prepared to play in Indianapolis.

2010 NCAA Men's Final Four Bracket

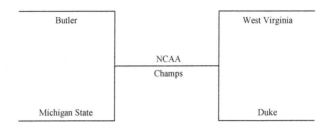

Just as four teams make it to the Final Four each season, there are four things that every person needs to understand about salvation. First, you are wonderfully and uniquely made (Psalm 139:14) by God, and God created a unique plan (Jeremiah 29:11) for your life. In his plan, the Creator of the universe wants to get to know you.

Second, you are separated from God when you consciously break one of the Ten Commandments. When you break one, you have actually broken them all. Everyone who has ever lived has experienced this sinful separation from God (Romans 3:23), and if you don't address it, spiritual death (Romans 6:23) will occur.

Third, God loved us so much that even while you and I were sinners (Romans 5:8), he sent Jesus to be the bridge over the sin that separates us from God. Jesus even bore our sin in his body when he went to the cross (1 Peter 2:24). But the good news that we celebrate every day is that Jesus rose from the grave on the third day (Matthew 28:6).

God arranged the first three steps. Now you must take the fourth step and decide to exchange your sinful life for a new life in Christ. You must repent, or turn from your sinful life, and ask God to forgive you (1 John 1:9). After you repent, you must place your trust in Christ and accept God's gift of grace that gives you eternal life (Ephesians 2:8), admitting that your salvation only comes through Jesus Christ (John 3:16). Obey God daily by praying and studying his Word to grow in Christ in all aspects of your life (Proverbs 3:6).

God offers everyone his free gift of grace. You can pray these words to receive Jesus Christ into your life as your Savior. Keep in mind that your attitude and change of heart are more important than these exact words.

Prayer: Lord Jesus, thank you for dying for my sins on the cross. Please forgive all of my sins through your blood that was shed for me. I am so sorry for my sins, and I believe that you died for me. Jesus, I ask you to come into my heart. Thank you for your grace that brings me eternal life in heaven. Thank you for the Holy Spirit who now lives in my heart. Thank you for accepting me as a child of God. In Jesus's holy name I pray. Amen.

Now consider these three statements one at a time. You cannot receive Jesus without admitting your sins and vowing to turn away from your sinful life. If you understand each statement and are willing to commit to each, you should pray and ask Christ into your life in your own words. Write your name under *saint*. You should receive the Holy Spirit and eternal life in heaven if you were sincere.

Heaven's Final Four

Step 1) God's Plan for Man

Psalm 139:14; Jeremiah 29:11

(Wonderfully Made; Plan for Good)

Step 3) Jesus Died for My Sin

Romans 5:8; 1 Peter 2:24; Matthew 28:6

(Loved sinner; My Sin His Body; Jesus is Risen)

Saint

Step 2) My Sinful Self

Exodus 20:3; Romans 3:23; Romans 6:23

(Self idol; All sinned; Apart from God)

Step 4) Repent, Trust, Obey

1 John 1:9; Eph. 2:8; John 3:16; Prov. 3:5-6

(Cleansed; Grace; Eternal Life; All Your Ways)

Check box if you sincerely intend to:

☐ Repent (turn from) all of your sin.

☐ Trust Jesus Christ as your Savior and Lord.

☐ Obey God by praying and studying his Word.

If you checked all three boxes, pray now for Jesus Christ to come into your heart. Write your name in the box under *saint*. Welcome to God's family as His child.

BK53
SWAPPING PINE TIME
FOR PRIME TIME!

Matthew 28:19–20, Acts 1:8,
1 Corinthians 9:24–27, 2 Timothy 4:2

I myself should become disqualified.

1 Corinthians 9:27

Deandre Liggins played the two (shooting guard) for the University of Kentucky Wildcats. During the 2008–2009 season, Deandre logged solid minutes as the Cats suffered through a decidedly sub-par season. Liggins showed signs of brilliance, but he often took bad shots and played out of control like a frisky colt. A new coach, John Calipari, and three sensational freshmen breathed new life into the 2009–2010 Wildcats, who were 25-1 and ranked second in the country. Obviously, three freshmen averaging double digits cut into the playing time of several returning lettermen, most notably Liggins.

One of the biggest surprises of the season was how far Liggins fell on the depth chart. The one thing that a basketball player wants more than anything is PT, playing time. After averaging sixteen minutes per game the previous season, Deandre did not play (DNP) in the first nine games. Every Division 1 basketball team has several walk-ons, and even the walk-ons played in the forty-point blowouts as Liggins rode the bench. Rock bottom came when Deandre sat against lowly Hartford. He had the same speed, quickness, jumping ability, and three-point shot as the previous season. So where was Deandre? Why wasn't he playing? Finally Cal played him against Indiana on December 12 for only one minute.

During the off-season, several players had transferred when the new coach and players came. As fall semester ended, Deandre must have been discouraged and surely considered transferring or quitting. But he stayed and didn't give up. In January, Deandre's playing time increased to twelve minutes per game. In February, it doubled to twenty-three. ESPN GameDay came to Lexington for Kentucky's biggest game of the season against Tennessee before a raucous Rupp Arena crowd and a national prime time audience. Liggins played a season-high twenty-eight minutes and responded with seven points, four assists, four rebounds, and several huge defensive plays, including a diving steal of a 50-50 ball that earned him a chest bump from Cal at midcourt.

Deandre swapped pine time for prime time. His inspired defense and experience paid huge dividends down the stretch as the Cats sought their eighth national title. Deandre *knows* what it is like to sit in the darkness at the end of the bench for over two months, and he practiced hard and followed his coach's instructions to earn his playing time.

Oswald Chambers taught in a *My Utmost for His Highest* devotion that God can choose to play us or bench us. Chambers shared that it is quite possible for God to set us aside if we are not of service to him. The Apostle Paul told the Corinthians that he never wanted to be in a position to be disqualified from sharing the gospel. Paul knew that when sin separated him from right standing with God, he would be DQ'ed (1 Corinthians 9:27) and miss opportunities to share Jesus Christ. Paul didn't want to miss one day sharing the gospel. In fact, Paul urged his fellow

Christians to preach Christ urgently under only two conditions: when it is convenient and when it is not (2 Timothy 4:2).

As Christians, God holds each of us responsible for sharing Christ with other people. If we don't follow his game plan, he won't use us. God constantly tries to get us to change so that we can go from darkness to light. As we emerge from darkness into the light, our emotions could range from humiliation and embarrassment to utter relief and joy. When we are on the same page, God gives us more and more playing time in prime time. He puts more opportunities in our path. When we capitalize on these chances, it is possible to get into a wonderful grace spiral that brings joy to our lives and helps God increase his kingdom (John 3:30). It can be as simple as letting our lights shine (Matthew 5:16). When we allow God's light to shine brightly in our lives, we attract others to him.

Just as Cal rewarded Deandre with a chest bump, when we give our all for the kingdom, God is pleased and excited and just wants to chest bump us!

Prayer: Holy Father, thank you for your infinite patience with me. I want more playing time in prime time, and I realize that I need to be obedient. Help me grow through prayer and Bible study so that I will see more opportunities to share my faith and shine my light. Give me playing time today to help further your kingdom, Lord. In Jesus's name. Amen.

Note: In 2011, an ESPN story broke that his eligibility was in question due to a former relationship with an AAU coach, and Liggins was eventually cleared to play. Deandre's diligence and perseverance paid off. He was selected in the second round of the 2011 NBA draft by the Orlando Magic.

BK54
TORN ALLEGIANCE

Matthew 6:24

You cannot serve God and mammon (money). (KJV)

Becca and I placed our daughters in quite a predicament the way we raised them. When we married in 1981, we owned strong allegiances to our respective flagship universities, UGA for me and UK for Becca. Kentucky won the 1978 national basketball championship, and UGA won the 1980 national football championship. She and I quickly agreed to root for each other's flagship program, which obviously was not a hard decision. Like their parents, Allison and Jillian became fervent UGA football and UK basketball fans. We have pictures of our girls in football stadiums and basketball arenas as we followed our teams around the Southeastern Conference.

Usually, the four of us attend the annual UK-UGA basketball game in Athens. The year 2009 was the eighth consecutive year that we had a daughter at UGA. Allison was there for the first four and Jillian for the last four. In 2007, when Jillian was a freshman, she sat with us at the game. I am incognito at these games, given my Bulldog lineage, but Becca is true Big Blue with a UK clicker shaker and plenty of swagger. In 2007, Jillian sat next to her mother, which made for a pressure cooker situation.

Remember the pressure cooker your mom or your grandmother had? There was a pressure gauge that you could adjust to let off steam. At this game, to her left were several thousand of Jillian's newest UGA friends screaming their heads off for the Dawgs. To her right was her blue-bleeding mother yelling for the Cats. Jillian usually cheers vociferously at games, but that night, she was so torn about who to cheer for that she sat motionless throughout the game. Georgia rallied to beat UK in overtime. When Jillian left the arena, her blood pressure must have been up twenty points, and her stomach was in knots. She was tense and miserable because she never cheered for either team. I felt badly for her because she was so torn. Jillian had truly been between a rock and a hard place. Similar feelings must be felt by parents who have strong allegiances to one school, and their child plays at the rival university.

The Georgia-Florida football game has forty thousand in red and black and forty thousand more in blue and orange. There is a continuous buzz of noise throughout the game, but obviously, one half of the stadium cheers a good play while the other half is silent. Everybody in that stadium made a choice. Nobody could possibly cheer emotionally and devote themselves to both teams.

Just as you cannot commit yourself completely to two teams, the Bible teaches us that you can't serve God and money and that the love of money is the root of all evil. When you begin to love your money and hold it too close to you, you cut off the love for giving and helping others that God wants you to have. When you are tight-fisted, you can't accept the blessings that God wants to put into your hands because they are closed. From personal experience, too little money or too much money is a huge distraction. Just enough money seems to do the trick. When money becomes our little g-o-d, or any stronghold is placed above God, realize that more of anything other than God never will be enough. When God is truly our God, he is all that we need.

Prayer: Father God, may I be committed to you and not my money. When I have too little or too much money, help me seek your guidance. May I freely give of my time and my money to help you grow your kingdom. In Jesus's holy name. Amen.

BK55
BRACKET BUSTERS

John 4:7–26, 5:1–9, 8:1–12, 9:1–14

This day when Jesus made the paste and healed his blindness was the Sabbath.

John 9:14

March Madness is one of my favorite events of the year. Office pools break out all over America, and productivity drops as workers track the scores of their favorite teams and sneak a peek at March Madness on demand. I fill out my Final Four bracket, as will millions of basketball fans who will try to pick the most winners, predict the teams that make it to the Final Four, and hope for a shot at a one-million-dollar prize with a perfect bracket.

It's funny how people who don't know basketball sometimes pick better brackets than the basketball junkies. The challenge is to pick the teams who will be the surprises of the tournament. The mass appeal of the tournament is fueled by the buzzer beater wins of the underdogs that upset the favorites.

Here is a brief tutorial for those who don't follow the NCAA tournament. Play begins with sixty-eight teams. Four play-in games reduce the field to sixty-four teams. There are sixteen teams seeded 1 (the strongest) through 16 (the weakest) in each of four geographic regions: East, South, Midwest, and West. In the first round, the 8 seed meets the 9 seed, the 7 seed plays the 10 seed, and so forth, with the 1 playing the 16. The experts call it an 8-9 game or a 7-10 game. A 12 upsetting a 5 is fairly common, and a 13 over a 4 or a 14 over a 3 happens occasionally. Only four times in twenty-five years has a 15 defeated a 2. The underdogs who pull off these stunning upsets are called bracket busters because they blow up your bracket after you picked a higher seed to advance.

But a 16 has never defeated a 1. The 16 seeds have a perfect 0-100 record in the first round. The closest call came when Princeton lost by one to Georgetown in 1989. Close, but no cigar. Below are the 1-16 matchups for the 2010 NCAA tournament: Kansas, Kentucky, Duke, and Syracuse, four of the top basketball programs of all time, versus Lehigh, E. Tenn. St., Vermont, and the University of Arkansas at Pine Bluff (a.k.a. UAPB). You can easily see what a mismatch these games are.

2010 NCAA Tournament

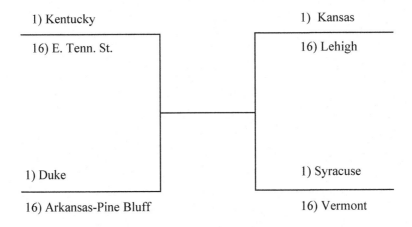

1) Kentucky

16) E. Tenn. St.

1) Duke

16) Arkansas-Pine Bluff

1) Kansas

16) Lehigh

1) Syracuse

16) Vermont

Just as the odds are highly stacked against the lowest seeded teams, the odds were highly stacked against the lowest seeded people of Jesus's day. Here is the way that the lowest seeds would have looked against the top seeds, who were the power brokers of the day.

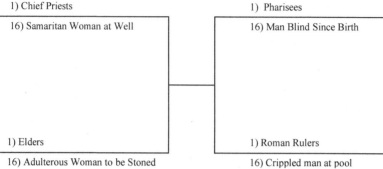

1) Chief Priests

16) Samaritan Woman at Well

1) Pharisees

16) Man Blind Since Birth

1) Elders

16) Adulterous Woman to be Stoned

1) Roman Rulers

16) Crippled man at pool

In a Jewish and Roman world that made outcasts of females, the weak, and the least fortunate, Jesus was the supernatural power behind these four bracket busters. Jesus asked the Samaritan woman for a drink of water and promised her living water if she would only believe. Not only that, but Jesus admitted to her that he was the Messiah, as she rightly guessed. At the Bethesda pool, Jesus raised up a man who had been crippled for thirty-eight years. Then Jesus made the mud paste and gave sight to a man who had been blind since birth. Not only that, but he did it on the Sabbath, which infuriated the Pharisees. Last but not least, Jesus drew in the dirt with his finger and told the self-righteous mob to throw the stones at the adulterous woman if any of them had never sinned. His action rescued the adulterous woman, and Jesus told her to sin no more. These two women and two men, all seemingly without hope, received the greatest upset victories of their lives. Through the love, kindness, and power of Jesus and the mercy and grace of God, countless others continue to have hope.

Prayer: Father God, thank you for sending us Jesus to give hope to the blind, the lame, the outcasts, and to all who have odds that appear to be insurmountable. Through your unconditional love, mercy, and grace, help me remember that all people have hope through Jesus Christ regardless of circumstance. In the holy name of Jesus. Amen.

BK56
GOD LOVES A CHEERFUL GIVER
(AND EVEN SELFISH ME)

Matthew 25:45, 2 Corinthians 9:7

God loves it when the giver delights in giving.

2 Corinthians 9:7 (MSG)

I flashed back to my mission trip with my church family to Cartago, Costa Rica. It was Tuesday afternoon, and suddenly, the temperature dropped about ten degrees, the skies darkened, and the rain poured down. Clouds would swoop in over the mountains into the valley with little warning. I learned to recognize that chilly air meant that rain was on the way. That afternoon, Pastor Danilo's son, David (pronounce Dah-veed), had been on a building supply run when he got caught in the downpour. When he walked into the shell of the church we were building, he was drenched from head to toe. I could see him shivering across the way. That is when I felt the urge of the Holy Spirit to help him. The inner conversation went something like this:

Holy Spirit: "I know that you see David shivering over there. Why, his teeth are chattering! Don't just stand there like a bump on a log. Give him the T-shirt that you are wearing. You have another one in the bag, but the one you have on will fit him. The other one is too small!"

Me: "No!" I said, clutching my University of Kentucky 7-time national champion T-shirt, a very prized possession.

Holy Spirit: "What do you mean, no? Do I need to hit you with a two-by-four? Take your shirt off your back and give it to David."

Me: "Oh, all right! I have learned in the past eight months that you won't leave me alone when I'm supposed to do something."

The T-shirt came off, and I handed it to David. He smiled broadly and said, "A million thanks!"

The next afternoon, David shows up at the work site and he has a gift for me. It's a brand-new shirt that he bought to replace the one that I gave him. He probably spent half a day's wages on it, and it has a great smell that masked the odor of my sweaty body. I could also use it to mask the odor of my sinful, selfish attitude from the day before. Boy, did I feel humble! Here I gave him an old, faded T-shirt for a brand-new shirt. Needless to say, I was completely touched by his generosity and gratitude. I proudly wore the new shirt to church Thursday night, where I gave my testimony to the congregation.

God loves a cheerful giver. He loves it when we help people less fortunate than ourselves. He also loves us when we don't cheerfully give. I seriously doubt that when I get to heaven and I receive my crown, there will be a jewel in the crown for my Wildcat T-shirt. But I learned an important lesson. When God prompts me to give, I don't want to waver. As believers, we have a close and personal Friend, the Holy Spirit, to remind us when we hesitate.

Prayer: Father God, thank you for the people of the Cartago church, who taught me so much about love and warmth during that mission trip. May all who read this devotion have a chance to experience the blessings that come from giving freely of themselves on a mission trip. In Jesus's name, I pray. Amen.

BK57
WE'RE READY TO FLY

1 Thessalonians 4:14–18, Revelation 21:1–5

Behold, the tabernacle of God is with man, and He will dwell with them, and they shall be His people.

Revelation 21:3

One of the rites of passage of college students on a major college campus is camping out to get tickets to an important conference game. The most famous example of camping out is K-Ville, or Krzyzewskiville, on the Duke campus. Each basketball season, hundreds of students will spend not days but weeks living in a tented village to get the best seats for upcoming games. You have gotta love basketball and your team to spend the night studying and sleeping in sub-freezing temperatures for a two-hour basketball game, but there is no denying the dedication and fervor of the Cameron Crazies. Love them or dislike them, they set the pace when it comes to the degree of hardship endured to be the first inside the arena to watch their team play.

Pastor Bert Neal showed us slides from his trip to the Holy Land. One slide in particular captured my attention. He took a picture of a graveyard with graves above the ground. Now that's common in New Orleans, which is below sea level, but these graves were on a hillside. The hillside was the Mount of Olives, so there were people who carried rocks several hundred feet up the hill to build these graves for their loved ones. The hillside is so crowded with an estimated one hundred fifty thousand graves that there is barely room to walk between the graves.

Why would anyone want to be buried on a hillside? There is a very good reason. The hillside faces the east gate of the Jerusalem wall, and these people believed that when Jesus comes back there will be a new heaven and a new earth. They believed that Jesus will enter the east gate of the new Jerusalem and they wanted to be the first ones to meet him and enter the gates triumphantly with him. First Thessalonians assures us that the bodies of those who went before us will leap from their graves and receive glorious, resurrected bodies like Jesus has.

FFH, a popular contemporary Christian band, wrote a song called "Ready to Fly." The day that Jesus comes back and we meet him in the clouds, we will be united with him forever. That event should be one cool, amazing sight, and while it is a little scary to think about how it will happen, rest assured we will be perfectly safe with Jesus.

Prayer: Father God, thank you for the strong faith of those early believers who not only believed Jesus was the Messiah but were so sure that he would return that they wanted to be first into the new heaven and new earth with him. In Jesus's holy name. Amen.

BK58
TAKING ONE FOR HIS TEAM

1 Peter 2:24

Who Himself bore our sins in His own body on the tree, that we, having died to sins, might live for righteousness, by whose stripes you were healed.

My coach friend and golf buddy A.G. Crockett shared this coaching story with me. I refereed several games for him in the 1980s, and I was familiar with the subjects of this story. Rockdale Co. played Dodge Co. for the Class AA girls state championship. Dodge scored with a few seconds remaining to take a one-point lead, and a Dodge player called a timeout. Unfortunately, her team was out of timeouts. Traci Waites was a three-time Parade All-American from Rockdale County and one of the great players in the history of the state of Georgia. Traci went to the line and made both free throws, and Rockdale won the state championship.

As you might imagine, the Dodge County girls were distraught, particularly the girl who lost her composure and called the extra timeout. To Dodge County Coach Dick Kelley's everlasting credit, he told reporters afterward that it was his fault and that he had told the player to call a TO. This wasn't true, but Dick couldn't stand the thought of a kid having to answer those questions, so he took the blame. In the midst of major disappointment and sadness, he took the mistake of his player and put it squarely on his shoulders. Who knows how much fruit has and will continue to come from that decision as those girls raise children and grandchildren?

I knew Dick around that time from local slow-pitch softball tournaments because Dodge County was adjacent to my home county of Laurens. The impact of that decision was such that Coach Crockett distinctly remembered the story almost thirty years later in 2009. A.G. wondered aloud how the seeds that were planted in those players and in the one player who called the timeout have flourished.

Just as the coach took the blame and placed it squarely on his shoulders, Jesus took one for his team. Jesus took all of our sins and placed them squarely on his shoulders at the cross. The verse 1 Peter 2:24 tells us that Jesus bore our sins in his own body on the tree, which is another name for the cross. Despite the weight of all future, past, and present sins and his Father turning his back on Jesus because of those sins, Christ managed to keep himself on that cross for three more hours after darkness came over the land. That's how much he loved us and loves us still.

Prayer: Father God, thank you for coaches who make the right decisions in the toughest situations. May we learn from this example when we have people to support who need us to take one for the team, just like Jesus took the ultimate one for us. In Jesus's name. Amen.

BK59
AGAIN

Ephesians 2:8–9, Romans 5:8, 1 Peter 2:24, Acts 2:4

Who Himself bore our sins in His own body on the tree...

1 Peter 2:24

The 2010 Sweet Sixteen Kentucky High School Athletic Association Boys Basketball Championship was played in fabled Rupp Arena. This state tournament is unique because there are no classifications, which means all high schools, large and small, compete to play in one tournament. Muhlenberg County High School endured a very turbulent ride to get there. Muhlenberg County, one of the most intense basketball counties in Kentucky, opened a new high school in 2009 following the consolidation of Muhlenberg North and Muhlenberg South, who were bitter archrivals. "Imagine Kentucky and Tennessee merging," Muhlenberg Coach Reggie Warford said. Warford encountered sometimes hostile criticism after he was hired as the new coach to come back to his home county from Pittsburgh. Coach Warford attempted to mesh North players, South players, and his two sons. He was not prepared for the mean-spirited language and fights between some of the players. Some parents and adults were also hostile toward each other. At the end of January, the Mustangs were an ordinary 12-9 team. The team improved in February and closed the regular season with an impressive rout against a tough rival. But when Warford entered the locker room after the game, three players had quit, including a standout sophomore.

That night, the Mustangs became a team. Afterward, the star player, Gabbard, hugged Warford and said, "Coach, this is our team now ... I'm going to get you to Rupp." The standout sophomore had second thoughts about quitting and, with the blessing of his teammates, came back, although he endured many wind sprints before rejoining the team. Gabbard and other players joined him in running those sprints, a gesture not lost on Warford, who remarked, "When I saw that, I told the other coaches, 'We're about to be something special.'"

I heard Dr. Charles Stanley explain the difference between mercy and grace. Mercy is not getting what you deserve, and grace is getting what you don't deserve. I gained further understanding of mercy and grace from an illustration by Jay Carty, author of *Coach Wooden: One-on-One*. My interpretation differs slightly from Jay's. The Muhlenberg player who quit the team was shown mercy by his coach and teammates by being allowed to come back. He still suffered the consequences of running many sprints, but when his teammates ran them with him, that was grace. Their love and forgiveness encouraged him to endure and forged a tighter bond among his teammates.

Muhlenberg's wind sprints reminded me of the classic scene in *Miracle*. In a pre-Olympic exhibition game in Norway, after Coach Herb Brooks saw his players giving a lackluster effort and checking out the girls in the stands, he snapped, "You guys don't wanna work during the game? No problem. We'll work now. Goal line. That one!" When the assistant coach blew the whistle, the team sprinted over and over from goal line to blue line and back, goal line to red line and back, goal line to the other blue line and back, and finally, from goal line to goal line. "Again." Whistle. "Again." Whistle. "Again."

"Herb, this is madness. Somebody's gonna get hurt!"

"Blow the whistle."

"Again!" Whistle.

After one hour, the arena lights were turned off by the maintenance crew, and the team sprinted in darkness for another hour. Finally, Mike Eruzione, who became team captain, got it. He told Herb that he played not for Boston University but for the USA. This weary group of prima donnas put aside their selfish interests and bitter college rivalries and became Team USA on the Norwegian ice.

Jesus Christ ran our sprints on the cross as he bore the heavy consequences of our transgressions. He paid the penalty for our sins. We didn't deserve his sacrifice, yet Jesus died for us while we were still sinners (Romans 5:8). But God loves us so much that he allowed his Son to hang for six hours on a cross in excruciating pain with railroad-type spikes driven through his hands and feet. In his holiness, God couldn't look upon the sin that Jesus represented, so God made the sky black. In those three hours of darkness, Jesus labored time and time again to take his next breath as he raked his torn and bleeding back on the rough wooden cross. Again. Again. Again. Why? Because Jesus loves each of us so much. Jesus died on the cross, arose from the grave, and appeared to his disciples, who still hadn't gotten it after three years of coaching. But when an average group of individuals received the Holy Spirit as Jesus had promised, they became the greatest twelve-man team the world has ever known. God gives each of us a choice to join his team by receiving his free gift of grace, which we cannot earn (Ephesians 2:8–9).

Prayer: Father God, thank you for the trials and life lessons that we learn from sports competition. May we use your wisdom, guidance, and instruction to make better teams wherever we work or study. In the name of the One who took our place. Amen..

BK60
ONE AND DONE

2 Corinthians 5:21, 1 Peter 2:24

For He has made Him to be sin for us, who knew no sin;
that we might be made in the righteousness of God in Him.

2 Corinthians 5:21

The expression "one and done" is a popular basketball term that has different meanings. First, when the offense shoots and misses and the defense gets the rebound, that's the end of the possession for the offense, which had one shot and only one shot. Too many "one and done" possessions will ultimately end a team's chance of winning the game.

"One and done" also describes an aspiring team's chances in a season-ending tournament such as NCAA March Madness. Some teams are "one and done" by early Thursday afternoon. It's as if they weren't even in the tournament.

The term "one and done" can also be used to refer to a college player who is so outstanding that he is drafted by the NBA after only one season, the freshman season. Carmelo Anthony, Derrick Rose, Tyreke Evans, John Wall, and Brandon Knight come to mind.

The ultimate "one and done" occurred when Jesus took the sins of the world from the garden of Gethsemane, dragged the cross on the Via Dolorosa, and ultimately was nailed to that cross.

After Jesus rose from the grave, the animal sacrifices that had been made for hundreds of years came to a screeching halt for thousands of Jews weeks after Jesus ascended to heaven.

The old covenant of animal sacrifices had been replaced by the new covenant. The blood sacrifices and the sprinkling of the doorposts would never have to be followed again because Jesus shed his own blood as the sign of God's new covenant with the people, first the Jews and later the Gentiles. Jesus Christ, who knew no sin but became sin for us so that we might become his righteousness (2 Corinthians 5:21), had delivered the ultimate "one and done."

Prayer: Most wonderful Father, I am so grateful that Jesus had the courage as the Son of Man and Son of God to deliver on a "one and done" for me. In Jesus's name. Amen.

BK61
SECOND CHANCES

Lamentations 3:22–23

> The steadfast love of the Lord never ceases, his mercies
> never come to an end. They are new every morning, great
> is your faithfulness.

A critical basketball statistic is second-chance points. The ability of a team to gather offensive rebounds and score put backs is a key stat in any contest. When the initial shot is missed, there is a scramble for the ball as the offensive and defensive teams attempt to gain possession. If the offensive player gets it, he or she will shoot the ball for the second time in that team's possession.

The more offensive rebounds the more second chance points that a team can score. Make enough second-chance points, and they will demoralize the opposition and give you a W that you might not have expected.

God usually gives you plenty of second chances to come to know Christ as Savior. After the first time you have a chance to receive Christ and reject him, usually second chances follow in the form of vacation Bible school teachers, pastors, Sunday school teachers, coaches, friends, and parents. Oftentimes, if your heart is hardened, you won't even realize that you passed on many chances. Nevertheless, God constantly puts these people in your path who will share the gospel and demonstrate the love of Christ. God chose to work through other people to advance his kingdom. That's how much trust God places in people who don't deserve the mercy and grace that he so freely gives.

But one day, the last second chance will come in this life, and after that, there will be no more second chances. Once this life passes, we will either be in heaven or in hell. If we are in hell, the Bible promises that there will be eternal torment, remorse, and regret. The remorse will be over all of the second chance opportunities that were missed and ignored. The next time you sense you have been given a second chance, capitalize on it and the gates of heaven will be yours. For eternity, you can celebrate the best decision you can ever make.

Prayer: Most gracious and forgiving God, I don't deserve the second chances, so I thank you for the many times you make it possible for me to accept your free gift of grace, which I could never earn. I am so grateful for your unconditional love, and may I honor you in all that I do. In Jesus's name. Amen.

BK62
PINE TIME IN PRIME TIME

Romans 8:28, Exodus 20:3, 1 John 1:9

And we know that all happens to us is working for our good, if we love God and are fitting into his plans.

Romans 8:28 (TLB)

When I was a high school senior, I discovered a passion when I refereed three middle school basketball games. I loved it. That day began an involvement with officiating that has lasted since 1972. I have long since retired from college basketball officiating, but I still referee our Hoops2Heaven high school games and enjoy training young officials.

After I refereed those three games on a Saturday, my West Laurens team played a weaker opponent, Johnson County (Herschel Walker's high school before his time), that evening. I had averaged about fourteen points and four or five assists per game. Most nights, I got my teammates involved in the scoring and my points would come in the flow of the game. But I decided before the game that I would topple my career high of twenty-three points. I thought a PR (personal record) would be a cinch because I had been shooting well all season. It would just be a matter of getting enough shots.

I rattled in a twenty-footer on our first possession. Hitting your first shot is usually a very good sign, but when I let it go, I had no wrist snap. I fired shots off the iron for the entire first quarter. Seven consecutive misses and several shots were forced. I clanged the rim like the bell of a San Francisco cable car approaching a stop. *Clang! Clang! Clang!* Coach Wildes rarely sat me, but he looked at me in the huddle and suggested very nicely, "Danny, why don't you sit with me for a few minutes?" In reality I benched myself with tired legs, a stiff wrist, and a swelled head! I hurt my team by selfishly going away from our game plan, and my reward was pine time in prime time. I finished with a season low six points as our team won by twenty.

God was, is, and always will be the Head Coach. When we get too big for our britches, he will let us sit on the pine (the bench) with him. We can't afford pine time because it is always prime time in the kingdom. We need to confess the specific sin, energize our prayer life and Bible study, and be ready when he chooses to put us back in the game. God will always forgive us after we admit our mistakes to him. He will remind us of the power of the Holy Spirit within us.

Sometimes, we force the action due to a lack of wisdom and discernment. If we share Christ in a way that isn't aligned with God's will, most likely it won't be effective. I recall several situations that I would have handled differently, but mistakes can teach us valuable lessons. If we allow God to work within us, he will reveal the proper approach and timing in his prime time.

Prayer: Father God, please give me a burning desire to share the good news in complete accordance with your plan and your timing. May I share the good news within the bounds of your eternal game plan. When I share from your game plan, I can be confident that you will bless my kingdom work mightily. In Jesus's name. Amen.

BK63
A TRIBUTE TO
COACH JOHN WOODEN

Psalm 119:100–105, Matthew 12:34, Ephesians 4:29

Drink deeply from good books, especially the Bible.

—John Wooden

John Wooden, who won ten NCAA men's basketball titles at UCLA, went to be with the Lord at the age of ninety-nine in 2010. Tribute after tribute praised him as a great man, coach, teacher, father, and husband. My fondest recollection of Coach Wooden is the devotion book that he co-authored with Jay Carty at the age of ninety-three. My niece Darla gave me the book for Christmas, and it became the first book of devotions that I read with regularity. It was a marvelous collection of sixty devotions and unknowingly might have been the seed that was sown that led me to write my sports devotion books. For that seed I am truly grateful. Here are my personal reflections on a man who was a great spokesman and servant of Jesus Christ.

When John was a boy in Indiana, he and his brother were playing in the barn when his brother threw manure in his face. He cursed his brother and went after him. His dad broke them up and whipped both of them, his brother for throwing manure and John for cursing. Coach Wooden said he never used profanity again in eighty-five years. Can you imagine going eighty-five days without cursing? His UCLA players knew Coach Wooden was really upset with them when he would stop practice and say, "Goodness gracious sakes alive!"

Coach Wooden and Press Maravich, Pete's father, had great respect for each other. Wooden thought that Press had a brilliant basketball mind but was too wrapped up in Pete's individual success. Plus, John would cringe when Press would let a good-natured string of expletives fly at the basketball camp at Campbell College. Each day, the coaches would each put a dollar in the pot, and if Press could go the entire day without cursing, the money would be his. He never collected. But surely John Wooden prayed often for Press to know his Savior and Lord personally, and twenty years later, Pete helped lead Press to Christ. Surely Coach Wooden rejoiced that he would meet his good friend, Press, and his prodigal son in heaven one day. Regarding the devotion book that Coach Wooden co-wrote, what a lesson we can learn from Coach Wooden becoming an author so late in life. When we are obedient to God, we can never tell where he is going to lead us and when he is going to do it. And that's where the real excitement in living occurs.

Coach Wooden once said, "I always tried to make clear that basketball is not the ultimate. It is of small importance in comparison to the total life we live. There is only one kind of life that truly wins, and that is the one that places faith in the hands of the Savior. Until that is done, we are on an aimless course that runs in circles and goes nowhere."

Prayer: Father God, thank you for the legacy of John Wooden, and may his legacy continue to bear fruit for the kingdom for the next ninety-nine years. In Jesus's holy name. Amen.

BK64
SPEAKING THE TRUTH

John 14:6

I am the Way, the Truth, and the Life...

We've been very blessed at summer basketball by a ten-year-old boy that I will call John. John is autistic, and from game to game, we're never quite sure what to expect. But our Hoops2Heaven ministry has never turned a child away who was physically able to play.

One of the highlights of the season was when John scored a basket, and the entire gym erupted in applause as his teammates congratulated him. There was also the day that John refused to play because our sports director, Michelle, placed a girl on his team and it just did not sit well with him. We made a quick adjustment, and the girl graciously moved to the other team without being offended. At halftime, when the devotions were given, there was no predicting what he would say and when he would say it. Sometimes, John would go on a tangent and take us off course from the message, and his mother and father would squirm anxiously in their seats.

But one night, when Michelle was presenting the devotion, John suddenly blurted out, "I told my friends at school that you need to believe in Jesus to go to heaven. People that don't believe in Jesus are going to hell." Michelle smiled and nodded and continued with the devotion.

The choice of heaven or hell is a truth that Michelle and I will carefully present in a loving way. Every child around him that evening might not have been ready to hear the truth the way that John presented it, but he had indeed spoken the truth. Every adult in the gym might not have been ready to hear it either. Jesus spent more time talking about hell than heaven, but we often take great pains to keep from pointing out the downside to people. John did it very clearly and succinctly, and I'm grateful to him that he had the belief in Christ and the presence to share with us.

Prayer: Most wonderful God Almighty, thank you for the truth that comes from the mouth of babes. In Jesus's name. Amen.

BK65:
FOLLOW WISDOM

Proverbs 9:10

The fear of God is the beginning of wisdom.

When I was in my late twenties, visions of greatness danced in my head. I had started a promising career as a college basketball official. I had cut my teeth on some easy small college games for a couple of years, and I began to branch out to get more experience. I attended a basketball official's camp at St. Joe's College in Rensselaer, Indiana, in the summer of 1983. The camp was operated by Dr. Henry "Hank" Nichols, the chair of the English department at Villanova University, the foremost college official of the era, and the referee in numerous NCAA championship games. I had developed pretty good judgment, hustled, and put a lot of flair into my calls; I was kind of a hot dog, frankly, which caught the eye of Nichols. He particularly liked the way that I mimicked his travel signal with a quick one rotation turn of the forearms and then pointing in the opposite direction.

On the final afternoon, Hank and Don Shea made me the referee in the camp championship game, which signified that I had been the top-rated official at the camp. While it wasn't the strongest group, one of my new friends, Terry McAulay, number 77, would later become an NFL official and would work two Super Bowls as the referee.

Before the final game, Hank did me a huge favor. He called me over and said, "Farr, go stand under the basket at the other end of the court. I am going over to talk to Bobby Cremins, the head basketball coach at Georgia Tech. I will point you out to him and recommend that he use you for scrimmages. That will get you some experience calling D-I ball. When you get back to Atlanta, call him this fall and remind him of the conversation." What a nice gesture. I was on cloud nine as I drove back to Kentucky to my in-laws' home, where Becca was staying while I was at camp.

What happened during the fall with Cremins and Georgia Tech? Well, not much because I never called him. Why? I don't know. Maybe I was too shy. But I probably thought, *I'll just do it my way.* Has that ever happened to you, someone gave you great advice or opened a door for you but you never walked through it? It happens with our relationship with God all the time when we insist on going our way instead of his way. When we are in touch with God's plan and listening for his guidance, he knows what is best for us. It's up to us to be obedient and follow his plan, which is always better than anything we can do on our own. God is for us. He's always using circumstances and other people and directing us to, "Go here. Go there." Find out where God is working and where he is pointing and follow his lead.

Prayer: Father God, thank you for the many doors that you open for us. You must shake your head in amazement when we fail to walk through doors you have opened for us. May I keep my eyes and ears open and recognize where you are at work. In Jesus's name. Amen.

BK66
PETE'S HOOK SHOT

Exodus 20:3

You shall have no other gods before Me.

The most famous play in the history of Stegeman Coliseum at the University of Georgia occurred on March 8, 1969. Before an overflow crowd of thirteen thousand, "Pistol Pete" Maravich rallied LSU from fifteen down in the second half with a series of long rainbow jumpers that would have been three-pointers if the three-point line had been in effect then. The game went to overtime, and Georgia was up by two and had possession with only twelve seconds remaining. All Georgia had to do was play keep away from the exhausted LSU players.

But suddenly, a Georgia guard took an ill-advised jump shot and missed. Pete grabbed the rebound, drove the length of the court, and scored to send the game to a second overtime. LSU pulled away in the second overtime, thanks to Pete's free throws and Georgia's cold shooting. There was no shot clock in 1969, so with about forty-five seconds left, Pete went into his *Showtime* dribbling routine, going between the legs and behind the back. Three Georgia players chased him but couldn't catch him.

Just before the buzzer to end the game, Pete threw up a forty-foot hook shot and ran off the court with his index finger in the air, just like Joe Namath leaving the field in Super Bowl III about six weeks earlier. The shot swished for his fifty-seventh and fifty-eighth points of the night. Pandemonium broke out. Immediately, the Georgia male cheerleaders ran after Pete, picked him up on their shoulders, and paraded him around the court to the pleasure of the Georgia fans and to the utter dismay of the Georgia players. Perhaps never before or since have the home team cheerleaders carried an opposing player in celebration around the floor. Such was the magical legend of the Pistol.

As one version of the story has been told, the famous hook shot would have never materialized if the player from Georgia had not tried to steal the spotlight from Pete. When we make selfish plays and take bad shots to increase our scoring total, we hurt our team's chances to win the game. Just as we should always put the team's best interests first, we should place God and others first and our interests last. If Georgia had won the game, there would have been plenty of credit to share all the way around. I believe that Georgia player has thought about that shot many times in the years following the game. I hope that a valuable life lesson came with it.

Prayer: Father God, thank you for the lessons of unselfishness that I can learn from the game of basketball. Forgive me when I am a ball hog in life and want things my way too often. In Jesus's name. Amen.

BK67
NOTHING BUT NET

John 21:3–8

Cast the net on the right side of the ship…

John 21:6

Larry Bird, Magic Johnson, and Michael Jordan are given credit for revitalizing the NBA during the 1980s and early 1990s. Their styles of play were different, but all three were tremendous leaders. Magic and Larry were friends but were made out to be big rivals.

In 1993 McDonald's sponsored a series of commercials that pitted Michael and Larry making trick shots in a game of horse. With each commercial, the shots became more outlandish.

Larry would shoot the basketball and say, "Off the roof, off the scoreboard, nothing but net." *Swish!*

Michael would shoot and say, "Off the car hood, off the tree, nothing but net." *Swish!*

The array of shots was outlandish for effect. There are many trick shots on YouTube that are nothing short of incredible. In 2010, two University of Georgia basketball players made quite a splash with their incredible repertoire of trick shots.

Jesus had an important "nothing but net" moment with his disciples just before he ascended to heaven. After he had risen from the grave and appeared on several occasions to his disciples, the disciples, who were experienced fishermen, fished all night and caught nothing. Jesus shouted, "Have you any fish?" When they said no, he instructed them to drop their net over the side of the boat. *An outlandish request,* Peter must have thought. "Nothing but net," Jesus told them. Just drop the net. Peter obeyed, and they caught so many fish, 153 to be exact, that the net almost burst.

Sometimes we feel that God makes outlandish requests of us. *You mean it's a sin if I just think bad thoughts? If I cheat on my homework or tell my friend a half-truth, that makes God angry?* God expects us to be perfect in the sense that he wants us to come clean when we do mess up, no matter how small the sin might be. Great rewards await those who stay clean by confessing their individual sins to God.

Prayer: Father God, I know that it is impossible to stay pure, and you and I know that I'm eventually going to slip. But help me give it my best shot, and thank you for disciplining me to help me be more like Christ. In Jesus's name. Amen.

BK68
WHO IS THAT KID?

2 Chronicles 34:1–3, Luke 2:40–52,
John 14:12, 1 Timothy 4:12

Did you not know I must be about my Father's business?

Luke 2:49

Twelve-year-old Pete Maravich was already a basketball camp veteran because his dad, Press, took him to every basketball camp that he worked during the summer. Even though Pete was small and frail, his skills were so advanced that he was winning free-throw shooting contests with college All-Americans such as Len Chappell of Wake Forest and scrimmaging with high school players. Soon, he would be dubbed "Pistol Pete" by a sportswriter who interviewed him after an eighth-grade game at Daniel High School in Clemson, South Carolina.

Young Pete was playing in a summer camp game with high school players as Bob Cousy watched from the sideline and chatted with a friend. Cousy was the NBA All-Star point guard of the 1959 world champion Boston Celtics. The "Cooz" was renowned for innovative moves such as his "wrap around the body" pass and an occasional behind-the-back dribble. Cousy was seemingly not paying much attention to the game as Pete came down the court with the ball. At midcourt, Pete threaded the needle with a forty-foot bounce pass through several players with some side spin. The ball ricocheted perfectly into the hands of his teammate for an easy layup. Cousy was so astounded by Pete's pass that he walked onto the court, *stopped the game*, and shouted, "Who is *that* kid?"

Little did Bob or anyone in the gym know that this twelve-year-old prodigy would become to the game of basketball what Elvis was to music. Pete would bring more originality and excitement to the game of basketball than had ever happened. "Pistol Pete" and his father, Press, took their entertaining brand of basketball called *Showtime* to the college basketball world in the late '60s, revolutionizing the game of basketball to this day.

Surely the priests, the Pharisees, and the most learned Jewish scholars of the day were equally astounded by a young prodigy named Jesus, who, at the age of twelve, shared incredible wisdom and insight as he preached in the temple. At some point, one of them must have turned to a friend and exclaimed, "Who is *that* kid?" Little did they know that they were watching and listening to Jesus, the Messiah, the long-awaited Savior of the world. Through the originality of his parables and miracles, Christ brought hope to the poor, to the downtrodden, to the oppressed, to women, and to all who longed for a better life. Many people in the temple failed to recognize that Jesus was the hope of a fallen world that had waited for the arrival of the Messiah for centuries.

Prayer: Oh God, thank you for the lessons that we can learn from our talented youth. May I encourage a youth with a special talent to strive to be all that he or she can be and remind them that Christ is always there to help. In the holy name of Jesus. Amen.

BK69
BUST THE CLOCK, COACH FARR!

Lamentations 3:22–23, Philippians 3:13–14

His mercies are new every morning.

Lamentations 3:23

In October 2012, I visited my dad, Coach Lester Farr Sr., who was four months shy of turning one hundred years old. To put that milestone into perspective, if a football field is one hundred yards long, Dad was sitting goal to go on the one-foot line, ready to punch it into the end zone!

During the era that Dad coached high school basketball from the 1930s to the 1970s, it was rare for one team to score one hundred points; so rare that the scoreboards of that era did not have room for a third digit. When a team scored one hundred points, the score would cycle from ninety-nine to double zero. The high school kids called it "busting the clock." In basketball terms, Dad has ninety-nine points and his free throw for number one hundred was in the air, and it was looking good!

He has taken great care of himself, and Coach Farr would be the first to admit that he has been remarkably blessed with good health through the years. However, the past year has revealed more signs of the inevitable aging process. Dad has been blind in his right eye for the past ten years, and macular degeneration has taken 90 percent of the sight in his left eye. Coach Farr wears hearing aids, but everything else works, which allows him to live by himself in his home with daily assistance from my brother, L.E., and my sister, Regina, who live nearby. He has a great appetite and thrives on a steady diet of Rice Krispies, bacon and tomato sandwiches, fried squash, and ice cream topped with strawberries.

Dad's short-term memory is fading, but he knows everybody's names and is still quick with a joke. Our daughter Allison took her new husband Kevin to meet Dad. The day before I asked Dad what advice he could share with the newlyweds since he and Mom were married for sixty-four years before she passed in 2003. Dad replied, "Give a little and take a little." I thought, *Good answer!* So I asked him the same question the following day as the four of us sat at the kitchen table. But this time, he quickly responded, "Be prepared to defend yourself." Ha!

Dad has maintained a wry sense of humor. Once he grimaced, and I asked him what was wrong. His reply? "Age."

Coach Farr still goes to church most Sunday mornings, pushing his walker up the church ramp more slowly but still saying the Lord's Prayer. He sleeps and catnaps about eighteen hours a day. It's almost impossible for him to generate activities that keep him sharp. However, L.E. asked me if I saw Dad counting on his fingers, and I had noticed. L.E. explained that Dad was counting the days until his one hundredth birthday. Obviously, he was motivated to get there!

Dad remarked that life was closing in on him. So I asked him what his attitude would be. Will you let one hundred close in on you, or will you close in on one hundred? After watching him take five laps with his walker through the den, living room, and dining room, I believe that he still has plenty of fight and determination, just like his basketball teams consistently demonstrated for thirty years.

Pray with me and my family that Coach Farr can keep straining to reach the end of his race (see Philippians 3:14), to one hundred and bust the clock for the glory of God! May his persistence and willingness to keep going each day inspire us to overcome the challenges which grow our faith

Update: Coach Farr celebrated his 100th birthday at his home with family and friends on February 10, 2013. He entered the pearly gates of heaven on April 16, 2014.

Prayer: Most gracious God, I praise you for every new morning that you give me and for every new morning that you give Coach Lester Farr. Give him the mercy, grace, and strength to keep going strong. May you receive the glory for his legacy of inspiration, determination and faith. In the name of Jesus. Amen.

BK70
FOUR CORNERS

Acts 10:8–15, 28–34, 45–48

Then he [Peter] became very hungry and wanted to eat; but while they made ready, he fell into a trance and saw heaven opened and an object like a great sheet bound at the *four corners*, descending to him and let down to the earth.

Acts 10:10–11

This devotion featuring Dean Smith, the legendary basketball coach of the University of North Carolina Tar Heels, and Kate Crockett, the daughter of Coach A.G. and Gayley Crockett, sister of John, and a 2010 UNC graduate, is offered to the glory of God in loving memory of Kate.

Kate was an avid Tar Heel fan and loved UNC just like her dad. She became good friends with another dean, the Dean of Admissions at UNC, after an impressive and relentless card-writing campaign to enter Chapel Hill. Her dream came true when he called one evening to grant her admission to Blue Heaven. I recall when Kate proudly called A.G. to tell him that senior Tyler Hansbrough was standing at her Chapel Hill bus stop!

After her graduation from UNC, Kate landed her dream job with a Manhattan publishing company, but less than a year later, she was diagnosed with cancer. For eighteen months, she waged an incredibly gutsy battle before she passed in August 2012. Dean

Smith coached a lot of All-Americans, including Michael Jordan and James Worthy, but he never had a player battle an opponent any harder than Kate fought cancer during her treatment period.

At the celebration of Kate's life, numerous tributes clearly illustrated how boldly she lived. She dearly loved her parents, her brother, her aunts and uncles, and her many close friends. Kate was a chip off the old block as she possessed a wonderfully wry sense of humor like her dad. She loved to have fun with people but not at their expense. Kate rolled with the punches with flair and class as evidenced by the grace that she displayed while playing one on one against Maya Moore, one of the greatest players in the history of women's basketball. One summer, Kate was matched against Maya before the entire camp at Reinhardt College. She earned the respect of her Milton High School teammates by making the best of a challenging and potentially humiliating situation, even making a three-pointer against Moore!

With respect to Coach Smith, he is the third winningest coach in college basketball history with 897 wins between 1965 and 1997 and captured two national championships. My favorite Dean Smith story is about the barber who was cutting a man's hair. The man in the chair gushed about rival Coach Norm Sloan's undefeated 1974 NC State national championship team, which upset UCLA and featured David Thompson, Monte Towe, and Tom Burleson. When the man finished gushing, the barber quipped, "Yeah, but just think what Dean could have done with that team!"

Coach Smith invented the "four corners" offense, which places an offensive player in each corner of the half court and features an elusive point guard who penetrates for layups or runs precious time off the court to preserve the lead. My favorite Tar Heel point guard was Phil Ford, who was peerless in the four corners and could spin dribble with the best of them.

Coach Smith fought hard on campus and in the community for African-Americans to receive the same treatment and opportunities as Caucasians. Seasoned Tar Heel fans recall that he signed the first black basketball player in ACC history in 1966. Charlie Scott became an All-American and enjoyed a stellar pro career with Phoenix and Boston.

Acts 10 features a story about overcoming the sin of prejudice. After being summoned to Joppa by a faithful Roman centurion named Cornelius, the apostle Peter envisioned four-footed creatures of every kind in a big sheet "bound at the four corners" and descending from heaven (10:11). After Peter refused to follow the Lord's command to eat the animals that were common and unclean (10:14), God revealed Peter's prejudice against Gentiles to Peter, who came to recognize that Gentiles were eligible for the saving grace of Jesus Christ just like his fellow Jews.

After speaking with Cornelius, Peter's breakthrough occurred. He said, "In truth, I perceive that God shows no partiality" (10:36). The Holy Spirit was poured out on the Gentiles (10:45), and Peter ordered the baptism of the Gentiles in the name of the Lord (10:48). Peter joined the apostle Paul in preaching the good news to the Gentiles. Even though he once denied Jesus three times in the courtyard, and therefore the rooster crowed, Peter preached with passion and led three thousand people to Christ in a single day!

Prayer: Most holy, gracious and loving God, we celebrate the saving grace of Jesus Christ, who favors no color, ethnicity, or nationality. Thank you so much for the inspirational legacies of your two Tar Heel children, Coach Smith and Kate Crockett, your child who touched so many lives in Georgia, North Carolina, New York City, and across the country. In the holy and wonderful name of Jesus. Amen.

BK71
A GOOD POINT GUARD
WILL FIND YOU

1 Peter 5:1–7

Let Him have all your worries and cares, for He is always thinking about you and watching everything that concerns you.

1 Peter 5:7 (TLB)

One of the most beautiful aspects of basketball is watching a master ball handler run the fast break. Not only does this type of player understand when to give up the ball, he also seems to know exactly where the other nine players are on the floor. Some of the best fast-break players include Bob Cousy, Magic Johnson, Steve Nash, and my all-time favorite, "Pistol Pete" Maravich. Pistol was a master of the fast break as he gave up the ball perfectly to players in front of him, beside him, and even behind him! Maravich had tremendous peripheral vision and even seemed to have eyes in the back of his head. He practiced so much with his LSU teammates that he understood where each one of them would be during the fast break. He could find them whenever he wanted to.

I hear occasionally that a person "found God" or "found Jesus." We never actually find God. God is never lost, so how can we find him? We may discover his presence and submit our lives to him in loving obedience, but God finds us. Wherever we are, God will find us. God is never lost, and he always knows where we are.

The Good News is that God tries to find us throughout our lives. He constantly pursues us to enter into a personal relationship with him. He loves us so much that he will never stop trying to find us, even if we don't seek him. Because the outcome of that search matters greatly to him for eternity, it should certainly matter to us. The least that we can do is to thank him constantly for his love and how he cares for us infinitely. Lost or found? It's our choice.

Prayer: Most loving and gracious God, thank you from the bottom of my heart that you love me so much that you would constantly pursue a right relationship with me so that I can spend eternity with you. In Jesus's holy name. Amen.

BK72
TIMELESS CLASSICS

John 1, 2 Timothy 3:16–17

All Scripture is given by inspiration of God, and is profitable for doctrine, for reproof, for correction, for instruction in righteousness, that the man of God may be complete, thoroughly equipped for every good work.

2 Timothy 3:16–17

I walked through the church parking lot on a Sunday morning as my friend Mark and his son Griffin got out of their car. Griffin had on my all-time favorite basketball shoes, the adidas Superstar, which came out in 1971. The classic three stripes and the reinforced shell toe was an exact duplicate of the shoe that I was so crazy about. I could tell that Griffin was extremely proud of his shoes, which were spotless. He said that he had bought them at Foot Locker after looking for them all week.

I teased him that those were my favorite shoes "back in the day," how my first pair had red stripes and my second pair had Carolina blue stripes. After I had my wisdom teeth removed, in my semi-coherent state, I asked my dad to drive to the sporting goods store to buy me another pair. It demonstrated that fashionable sneakers were constantly on my mind. Griffin seemed to enjoy my story, and we bonded over our mutual admiration of these classic shoes.

Later that morning, I told his mom Lisa about our "back in the day" conversation about the shoes. Lisa laughed and shared a comment that Griffin made the previous Sunday after our pastor told a joke about a young preacher. As the congregation laughed at the joke, Griffin deadpanned, "That joke is for old people." Yet Griffin was wearing old people's shoes, and he thought those were cool. When he bought them, he was likely unaware that he had just bought "old people's shoes."

It occurred to me that so many people think of the Bible as "an old people's book." Many people consider the Bible irrelevant because it was written thousands of years ago. How can a book written so long ago possibly be relevant today? It is relevant because it is the inspired word of God and the eternal Truth for the Ages. If you believe the Bible is true, how do you make it relevant? Open the good book and read it daily. As you learn the contents, God will show you its relevance to your daily life. If you will seriously commit yourself to daily reading and study, the Bible will become the timeless classic in your life. Allow God to help you today through his timeless word.

Prayer: Dear Lord, I know in my heart that the most timeless classic of all time is Jesus Christ, who never goes out of style. Father, thank you that you loved us so much that you sent Jesus from heaven to earth to die for our sins and bring us the hope of eternal life. In Jesus's name. Amen.

BK73
HOW IS YOUR FOLLOW THROUGH?

Ephesians 6:10–20

And take the helmet of salvation, and the sword of the Spirit, which is God's word; praying always with all prayer and supplication to the Spirit.

Ephesians 6:17–18

When Pete Maravich was a young boy in Clemson, South Carolina, he slept with his basketball every night. After his mother, Helen, tucked him in, kissed him good night, and left the room, Pete would pick up his basketball in the dim light. Lying on his back, he would take his shooting position, straight elbow with his wrist cocked. Over and over, sometimes for an entire hour, he would shoot the ball into the air and repeat, "Fingertip control, backspin, follow through. Fingertip control, backspin, follow through." His dad and coach Press taught him to point his index finger at the basket on his follow through to be an accurate shooter. The best way to shoot the ball was to use fingertip control, backspin, and follow through.

Oftentimes, we leave church all fired up with a renewed determination to share Christ with others, but by the time Monday comes, our follow through has fizzled. Often we are in a great position to share Christ with others, but we never actually follow through. When we are in position, we need to ensure that we have prepared our hearts so that the Holy Spirit can work through us. *Bible study, prayer, follow through. Bible study, prayer, follow through.* When we repeat these sequences daily, confessing our sin and asking God to forgive us, we will be prepared to take aim and follow through effectively for the kingdom. "That I may speak [the gospel] boldly as I ought to speak" (Ephesians 6:20).

Prayer: Most gracious God, thank you for sending Jesus to save us. Help me realize that I cannot help the kingdom by simply hoping that someone will come to Jesus. I must be ready because this is the day that you may choose to use me to bring someone to Christ. In Jesus's name. Amen.

BK74
ARE YOU REALLY GETTING AWAY WITH ONE?

1 John 1:7–9

But if we walk in the light as he is in the light, we have fellowship with one another, and the blood of Jesus Christ cleanses us from all sin.

1 John 1:7

Ryon Riggins, my young brother in Christ, is six feet nine inches tall and a talented college basketball player. I watched Ryon play basketball as a high school senior. A player drove to the basket, and Ryon slapped him on the arm as he attempted to block his shot. Even though you could hear the slap to the top row of the gym, the three referees failed to make the call.

His mom Rosalynne turned to me and Becca and said, "Ryon got away with one." I replied, "When I refereed, I called that the 'bacon frying' because you could hear the sizzle." You didn't even need to see the foul to make the call. You could call it simply by hearing the contact.

When is the last time that you committed a sin and felt like you "got away with it?" You didn't get caught committing the sin, and there were no repercussions. It could have been claiming a questionable tax deduction, or the misuse of resources at work or school, or a white lie, or cheating on an exam, or a snappy remark that embarrassed someone, but no one reprimanded you. The anxiety and danger passed, and you breathed a sigh of relief. But you didn't really get away with one because God saw it.

That uneasy feeling in your gut and the nagging presence of the action on your mind is called conviction, and it is brought on by the Holy Spirit that lives within believers. The closer that you are to God, the more acutely the Holy Spirit makes you aware when you commit a foul. Confess it immediately to God and to the person you fouled, and God will forgive you of the sin and wipe your slate clean.

Prayer: Father God, help me keep my slate clean by humbly confessing to you and to the person that I hurt. Thank you for always restoring me to a complete relationship when I confess my sin. In the holy name of our precious Savior. Amen.

BK75
GOD WILL NEVER LET YOU DOWN

Proverbs 18:24, 1 Peter 5:7, Hebrews 13:5, 8

There are friends who pretend to be friends, but there is a Friend who sticks closer than a brother.

Proverbs 18:24

Has anyone ever disappointed you? Has anyone ever let you down? I flashed back to the first basketball game that I saw my idol, "Pistol Pete", play. Pete was traded after the 1973–1974 season by the Atlanta Hawks to the expansion New Orleans Jazz. In late 1974, Pete was going through a very dark time in his life. His dad, Press, had been fired by LSU, his mother had tragically committed suicide in October, and the Jazz had a terrible 1–14 record. Their only win came when Pete hit a buzzer beater from the deep corner to beat Portland by one.

I drove from Athens to Atlanta in December to watch Pete in the Omni, expecting him to go for thirty or forty, make some terrific passes, and vanquish the Hawks. This game was Pete's first against Atlanta since the trade, and I am sure that he was anxious to have a big game against his former team. Perched expectantly on the edge of my seat near midcourt about five rows up, I squirmed as Pete had a miserable first half. He shot only four for fifteen as the Hawks opened a sizeable lead. Pistol continued to fire blanks in the third quarter. After missing another jump shot, he was called for an over the back foul on the rebound. Pete's frustration exploded like a powder keg. He charged referee Jim Capers, who called a technical foul as Pete continued to scream at him. As he got in the referee's face, Pete's left arm accidentally struck his lanyard, and you could see his whistle flip into the air. Capers had no choice but to eject Pete. Teammate Nate Witherspoon wrestled Pete off the court and dragged him toward the exit to the locker room. Pete continued to scream at Capers over Witherspoon's shoulder as they disappeared into the tunnel. The Omni crowd was surreally quiet because many fans had come to see Pete's return. I was stunned, literally speechless, and beyond disappointment. Pete had really let me down. I watched the remainder of the game in a disinterested fog because my idol had crashed and burned right before my eyes the first time that I ever saw him play in person! Pete was at the center of my existence. When he crashed and burned, I went down with him. It was a long, sad drive back to Athens.

Everyone and everything that we know, whether it be a spouse, child, family member, friend, coworker, classmate, boyfriend, girlfriend, or even a sports team, will eventually fail to meet our expectations. Some will fail us far more often than others, possibly leading to abusive situations that can damage our psyches. The closer that we place anyone other than Christ to the center of our lives, the harder the fall and the deeper the hurt when that human being fails us. The Bible teaches us that "All have sinned and fallen short of the glory of God" (Romans 3:23). When we put all of our eggs in one basket and make that basket the center of our focus, disappointment, hurt, heartbreak or bitterness can leave us despondent. There can seem to be little or no hope.

But the hope is that there is a friend who will never fail us, and that friend is God through a personal relationship with his Son, Jesus Christ. God promised that he will "never leave us nor forsake us" (Hebrews 13:5), and God and his Son are the same "yesterday, today, and forever" (Hebrews 13:8, KJV). God loves us perfectly every day. His love is immeasurable, infinite, and everlasting. God's love is always stronger than the love that any person can give. No one can comprehend the depth of God's love, which was best illustrated through the life of Jesus Christ, the Son of God and Son of Man.

I can imagine God looking at Jesus, sitting to his right, and saying, "Son, I need you to go live among our people and experience every negative emotion, hurt, and rejection that they will ever feel. Then, I need you to demonstrate the depth of our love by dying an incredibly painful death on a cross for their sins." Jesus loved those who came before us, and loves us, so much that he carried out his Father's plan perfectly.

The next time that you fall into despair, bitterness, and frustration over somebody or some team, make sure your relationship with Christ is in order. Through a strong relationship with Jesus Christ, you are in position to rest in his everlasting arms, allow him to heal you, and bring you back from your disappointment. You can trust God completely, and the Friend that sticks closer than a brother (Proverbs 18:24) is none other than Jesus Christ, our Savior and Lord.

Prayer: Father God, thank you for your perfect promise that you will never forsake me. May I place Christ at the center of my existence and know that whatever I have experienced or will experience, Jesus has already walked in my footsteps and knows exactly what I'm going through. May I rest in your perfect love and receive comfort, solace, and healing from my disappointments. In Jesus's name I pray. Amen.

BK76
TRUST THE REBOUND

Proverbs 3:5–6, Acts 2:4

Trust the Lord with all your heart, and do not rely on your
own understanding.

Proverbs 3:5

Bill Russell led the Boston Celtics to an incredible ten NBA
championships over a twelve-year span. Russell was never a great
scorer, but only because he chose to focus on preventing baskets.
He was an amazing shot blocker and would often deflect the ball
to a teammate instead of merely swatting it out of bounds. Bill was
also one of the greatest rebounders in the history of basketball. He
once garnered an astounding forty rebounds in one game. Not
only was he a tremendous leaper with long arms, but he had an
uncanny knack of anticipating which way the ball would bounce
off the rim.

The greatest rebounders study game film to determine where
the basketball is apt to bounce when it comes from a particular
direction. For example, a shot that is missed from the wing will
most often go to the other side of the basket. Therefore the great
rebounders will trust that the ball will go long more often than
short.

Great "faith" rebounders learn from their disappointments
and tribulations. They remember how God brought them through

their problems and how often he has done it. They believe that there is always a rebound or a bounce back after a period in the valley. When they get into a predicament or a jam, these faithful believers "trust the rebound" will occur.

Faith rebounders remember that God was with them in the valley as well as on the mountaintop. They trust that God's love is so great that he will see them through this challenge, and the next one and the next one after that. They don't know exactly when the rebound will occur, but they trust that it will eventually happen. Walking with God in obedience and being filled with the Holy Spirit (Acts 2:4) only serves to strengthen their resolve.

I keep a journal of prayer requests. When God answers a prayer request, I place a star beside the journal entry. It helps me see how faithful and consistent that God is time and time again! When I look back at the stars, I note that some are related to setbacks that he helped me overcome. Those stars constitute the rebounds. Perhaps remembering your deliverances will help you trust the rebound during your next crisis.

Prayer: Father God, your love and compassion for me in times of trouble become evident when you help me rebound from disappointment and heartache. May my faith grow as I trust the rebound. In Jesus's name. Amen.

BK77
HEAT CHECK

Revelation 3:14–20

Neither hot nor cold.

Revelation 3:16

A term called "heat check" is part of basketball jargon. An outstanding shooter will get into a zone and drain shot after shot, no matter what type of shot it is. The next trip down the court, the player thinks that he is so hot that he can make anything, so he fires up a thirty-footer. That shot is the heat check shot to see if he is so hot that he can truly make anything.

When Pete Maravich played for LSU, he would occasionally shoot forty-foot set shots. Pete would take one step across half-court, set his feet, and let it fly. Against one opponent he made a forty-footer, and the crowd went crazy. The next trip down the court he made another forty-footer. As former LSU football star and eyewitness Tommy Casanova shared in Mike Towle's book, *I Remember Pete Maravich*, "Pete was going to keep shooting it until he missed. The third trip down Pete let it fly. The ball rattled off the rim and the backboard, went halfway down, and spun out." That was Pete's heat check shot. After that he took normal shots. Actually normal for Pete was not normal for anyone else!

If you took a heat check of your faith, where would your spiritual temperature register during worship? Perhaps it would be pretty high. How is your spiritual temperature at home, work, or school? Most of us have varying degrees of warmth and Christian love in different facets of our lives. Christians should take occasional "heat checks" to ensure that all areas of our lives are registering consistently on God's heat check scale no matter where we are or what we're doing. To shine our light regardless of circumstance is the essence of displaying vibrant Christian love!

Prayer: Father God, I confess that sometimes I can be lukewarm or even cold for you depending upon my mood. May I take a heat check when I am out of sorts, confess my selfishness, and restore my fire for you again. In Jesus's name. Amen.

BK78
MY GO-TO

Psalm 142:1–2, Matthew 11:28, Romans 8:34

It is Christ who died, and furthermore is also risen, who is
even at the right hand of God, who also makes intercession
for us.

Romans 8:34

The favorite online blog of many University of Kentucky basketball
fans is *Kentucky Sports Radio*, a.k.a. KSR, at kentuckysportsradio.
com. Louisville attorney Matt Jones and his KSR blogging staff
post daily updates with everything you want to know, and then
some, about the Wildcats.

This quote appeared on a KSR blog after a loss to Florida.
"Neither player [Terrence Jones and Brandon Knight] was
perfect…, but seeing them take over the game when Kentucky
needed them to step up was a major step forward for a team that
has seemed to struggle in finding that go-to person at times."

In January 2010, UK fans saw their beloved Wildcats lose two
road games and fall into third place in the SEC East standings.
The outcome of each game was decided on a last-second shot by
a go-to player. Ole Miss senior point guard Chris Warren drained
a step-back, twenty-six-footer with two seconds remaining to give
Ole Miss the win. Four nights later, Brandon Knight, Kentucky's
freshman point guard, missed a twenty-five-footer with two

seconds to play as Florida held on for the victory. When the go-to player takes the shot, even if he misses, I'm much more satisfied with the outcome than if a lesser skilled player took the shot.

What is a go-to player? Every successful team has a player that when the pressure is on, you want the ball to go-to that player. A go-to player comes through in the clutch much more often than the average player, but it is humanly impossible to come through every time. Whether it is a sports team, the workplace, a church building committee, or a family, you need a go-to person that you can depend on to get the job done when you need it most.

Jesus Christ is our ultimate go-to person. On earth, Jesus often said that "I do what my Father asks of me." He is sinless and perfect. Jesus always came through for God as his go-to, and he always comes through for us. Most of all, Jesus came through when he paid the penalty for our sins by *going to* a horrific death on the cross. After his resurrection from death and his ascension to heaven, Jesus has served as our go-to advocate and intercessor to God our Father for almost two thousand years. When things are going well, and especially in times of trouble, we need to go-to him constantly for help. The evil one tries to get us to dwell on our problems and wants us to go-to anybody but Jesus to stop us from getting the best. Jesus is the one that will go-to the Father for us no matter how badly we've messed up. That's why we go-to the Father in prayer in the name of Jesus.

Prayer: Father God, help me to remember that Jesus Christ is my "go-to" no matter what my circumstances may be. Thank you that he always comes through when the chips are down. In Jesus's name. Amen.

BK79
PLAY EVERY POSSESSION

Colossians 3:1–17

Whatever you do, in word or deed, do everything in the name of the Lord Jesus.

Colossians 3:17 (KJV)

It was a frustrating 2010–2011 SEC campaign for Coach John Calipari's young UK squad because of their inability to win conference games on the road. Cal lost five players to the NBA from the 2009–2010 team, and he started three freshmen and only played a six or seven man rotation most nights. The Cats were undefeated at home, but lost six games on the road by four or fewer points. Several times they led in the second half only to hit a dry spell for several minutes, allowing their opponents to make a run that created a deficit they couldn't overcome.

Cal said that his team played great for thirty-five minutes, but for the other five minutes, they dug themselves a hole by missing defensive assignments, creating turnovers, or taking bad shots.

What he told his young squad time and time again is to forget the score and simply "play every possession." Consider that there are over one hundred possessions in a basketball game worth up to three points each. In a one or two point game, one possession squandered on offense or one mistake on defense can mean the difference in winning or losing.

God doesn't expect us to take off any possessions either. "Whatever you do, in word or deed, do *everything* in the name of the Lord Jesus" (Colossians 3:17, KJV). We go through hundreds of possessions daily in thoughts, words, or deeds. A great day's activity can be spoiled when we lose our temper, say the wrong thing, or cave into the temptation the evil one places before us. With God's help and strength from his mighty word, we can keep from making the crucial turnover that we later regret.

Prayer: Dear Lord, help me strive to complete every play, because I never know the play that could change someone's life for eternity. In the holy and perfect name of Jesus. Amen.

BK80
I KNOW THE FINAL SCORE!

Revelation 21:1–4

I saw a new heaven and a new earth.

Revelation 21:1

I held a book signing in Dublin, Georgia, the area where I grew up. The 2012 Kentucky–Florida SEC Tournament men's semifinal game was played in the middle of my signing, so I couldn't watch the broadcast. I asked my sister-in-law Gail to record the game for me.

During a lull, I accessed the live blog on Kentucky Sports Radio to follow the play-by-play by Matt Jones. The live blog is interspersed with comments from some very creative fans. You can certainly tell when UK is playing well and when they are not from the comments on the blog! UK held on late to win the game, and I breathed a sigh of relief.

The signing went very well, and I enjoyed meeting old friends and making new ones. That evening, I went over to my brother L.E. and Gail's house to watch the second half of the recorded game.

Even the recorded game was very exciting. The game was very physical. After Kentucky fell behind in the second half on a couple of borderline calls and Florida had a couple of three-pointers rim out, I was glad that I knew the outcome. Otherwise, I would have fretted big time and become upset about the calls.

With about thirty seconds left in the game and UK up by two, the recording malfunctioned. Gail felt badly about the malfunction and struggled to bring up the last portion of the game on the DVR. In her mind, the game hung in the balance because she did not know the final score. To relieve her anxiety, I said, "If you can't find it, it's okay. I know the final score."

Our reactions were different because I knew the final score, and she didn't. As followers of Christ we have a huge advantage. We know how the game of life ends because the Bible tells us that Christ defeated death. As believers, we will defeat death, and we will live with him forever in heaven.

When unpleasant surprises happen in our daily lives, Christ followers should not get as upset because we know things will play out just fine in the long run. We know the final score, and that Christ has assured us of victory!

Prayer: Father God, may I take what happens to me today in stride as calmly as watching a recording of a game. I know the ultimate outcome, which includes me meeting Jesus face-to-face. That will be so much more exciting than any game could ever be. In the holy name of our Savior and Lord, Jesus Christ. Amen.

BK81
LIFE LESSONS FROM THE
FINAL FOUR (PART 1)

Proverbs 10:1–14; 31–32

The mouth of the righteous brings forth wisdom, but the perverse tongue will be cut out.

Proverbs 10:31

Becca, Allison, Jillian, and I drove thirteen hours to Houston to watch our beloved Kentucky Wildcats in the 2011 Final Four. Unfortunately, the Wildcats lost to UConn by one point, 56–55, in the semifinal game at Reliant Park before a record Final Four crowd of more than 75,000 fans.

Our pregame excitement and anticipation was suddenly replaced by the disappointment of missing the championship game. Our plans and hopes were derailed. Instead of enjoying the sights and sounds of Houston and waiting eagerly for the Monday night showdown, I tried unsuccessfully to unload our four Monday night tickets at the NCAA fan to fan ticket window. We took the long walk back to our car in an outer parking lot.

Now we searched for a good meal to soothe the misery of seeing our team lose a game in which they had shot the ball poorly. I had not eaten since the beginning of the Butler–VCU game five hours ago, and I was very thirsty. *I should have gotten something to eat between games*, I lamented.

We waited seemingly forever in traffic to get back to the interstate that would take us to our downtown hotel eight miles away. As we sat at a red light near our hotel, a loud siren unexpectedly pierced the air. A policeman on a motorcycle whizzed by my door. He drove into the middle of the intersection and cordoned a path for an oncoming vehicle.

The light turned green, and I was faced with a decision. Do I go, or do I stay? A driver behind me blasted a very loud horn! No suggestions were forthcoming from inside the car. Backseat drivers, where is your help when I need it most? I dashed into the intersection and turned left. I sensed that I was in harm's way as a second policeman on a motorcycle sped by me escorting the vehicle.

Nervously, I jammed the gas pedal to avoid the motorcycles and whatever was on my bumper. I veered quickly into a small parking lot to the right and breathed a big sigh of relief. Whew, that was close! I glanced to my left and saw a big blue bus… with "Kentucky Basketball" on the front fender. It was the UK team bus on the way to the Hilton Hotel! We drove almost eight hundred miles to Houston, only to be totally disappointed when UK lost, and we almost got run over by the team bus!

After struggling to find a restaurant, we finally gave up and pulled into a McDonald's drive-thru. That is when my ugliness burst out. Having made curt replies in the car ever since I left the NCAA ticket booth, I was tired of driving in a city where I didn't know my way around. I was irritable, angry, frustrated, hungry, and thirsty.

Trying to relay four separate orders to an employee who was having trouble following me, I abruptly said, "Just forget it," and childishly drove away. Deservedly, I got the full brunt of it in the car from the other three famished family members. My ugliness had erupted, and I felt ashamed and embarrassed.

"Let's just go inside and place our orders," I said. But the restaurant was locked, and only the drive-thru was open! Sheepishly, I went through the drive-thru for the second time, and Jillian did a great job of summarizing our orders. We ate our lukewarm burgers and fries in our hotel room as we replayed the shortcomings of the game.

Prayer: Father God, I had no excuse for acting so ugly. I thank you for your forgiveness which you gave me after I made a fool of myself in front of my family, the drive-thru attendant, and you. Thank you for all of the times you forgive me when I don't deserve it. In the name of Jesus who died for me. Amen.

BK82
LIFE LESSONS FROM THE
FINAL FOUR (PART 2)

Proverbs 19:17, Acts 20:35

When you help the poor, you are lending to the Lord. And
He pays wonderful interest on your loan!

Proverbs 19:17 (TLB)

Early Sunday morning after UK's disappointing loss the previous
night, I walked to the team hotels to unload the tickets, but I
had no luck. No one wanted uppers (upper-level tickets), and the
people with uppers were trying to buy lowers (lower-level tickets).
I called two work associates in Houston to see if they could use
the tickets, but they weren't home.

Becca came up with a wonderful idea to give the tickets to
Houston policemen or firemen. Before taking Allison to the
airport to catch her flight, we headed for the nearest precinct
about ten minutes from the hotel.

After a wrong turn, we found ourselves in front of the massive
Second Baptist Church of Houston. I asked the policeman
directing traffic where the nearest fire station was, and he said he
didn't know. Inwardly I smirked, "One of Houston's finest doesn't
know where the nearest fire station is?" My attitude still needed
plenty of work.

I pulled into a small shopping center parking lot as Becca searched for the fire station location on her mobile phone. In an adjacent smaller parking lot sat a security attendant in a golf cart. Becca explained our predicament to him. He was extremely helpful and explained that the fire station was about a mile away on our left.

Becca thanked him, and the following observations came from one of the girls in the back seat. "He was really nice. Why don't we offer him tickets?" We all agreed. I parked the car and walked to his golf cart.

He was a gentleman in his late fifties, but the years had taken their toll on him. I explained how we were in town for the Final Four, how our team had lost, and that we were headed back to Atlanta. When I asked him if he would like to have two tickets to the final game, he instantly beamed and gushed, "I can't believe it! Nothing like this has ever happened to me. I'm going to call my mama and tell her about this. I came down here after Hurricane Katrina. Bless you. Bless you!" He chatted about how he had watched the games the previous evening, how he enjoyed watching the Kentucky team, and that he was now pulling for Butler. *Right answer*, I thought, since UK had lost to UConn.

As this wonderful man spoke, I literally felt God flip my attitude upside down. A warm glow engulfed me like a wave from his sincere and enthusiastic appreciation and gratitude. Suddenly, the bitterness of the past twelve hours melted. With his reference to Hurricane Katrina, it is reasonable to assume that the gentleman had come from the New Orleans area. Quite possibly he was one of the thousands of people who were moved by bus from NOLA to Houston. For him to want to call his mother about a couple of basketball tickets, perhaps it had been a monumental struggle for him ever since he had arrived in Houston in 2005. Perhaps he no longer envisioned opportunities such as attending the first NCAA championship game in Houston since the early 1970s. When I described his response to Becca, Allison, and Jillian, they were all delighted that we had given him the tickets. As I backed out of the parking spot, the gentleman drove his golf cart over and stepped out.

As Becca rolled down the window, he said, "I appreciate these tickets so much. I will tell everybody that I know how I got them, and I will be thinking of you all of the time that I am at the game!" Later, I was so pleased that he came over because my entire family received a similar blessing that I had received. I thought, *That fellow has got be a UK fan for life now.*

Becca is superb at directions, but we took a wrong turn that morning. I believe God arranged for our "impromptu" meeting to happen. Perhaps he saw a humble and gracious servant who needed a lift. God also saw the individual "needs" in our car. He saw me in need of an attitude adjustment as I thought about the upcoming thirteen-and-a-half-hour drive. He saw Becca talking about unfair writers and bad calls, including Josh Harrellson's second foul. That was the one that I disagreed with so demonstratively that I almost fell in the lap of the fan in front of me. Jillian was dreading Monday morning when she would return to her shorthanded office to face potential fire drills instead of cheering for UK at the national championship game. Allison was anxious about her return to class at Emory University because one of her group projects was not going smoothly. God rearranged everybody's perspective through this wonderful gentleman, a person who had so much less materially but was so rich in spirit.

From the New Testament teachings of Paul, Jesus taught his disciples that it is indeed more blessed to give than receive (Acts 20:35). From the Old Testament, Proverbs 19:17 (TLB) states, "When you help the poor, you are lending to the Lord. And he pays wonderful interest on your loan!" We made a small effort to help some people. But God repaid us in a way that will keep on giving. Whenever we think of Houston and our first Final Four as a family, it will be about how we traded our tickets for the lifelong memory of a grateful saint. I look forward to seeing my friend from Houston in heaven and asking him how he liked the game.

Prayer: Dear Lord, I can't wait to meet that wonderful saint from Houston in heaven. You melted my anger and frustration through a simple encounter with a person who has enjoyed far fewer privileges and has gone through many more struggles than me. Thank you for the gratitude check. In Jesus's name. Amen.

BK83
A WHITE MAN CAN JUMP

John 11

He cried with a loud voice, "Lazarus, come forth!"

John 11:43

Jacob Tucker is living proof that at least one white man can jump high. Really high! He made a big splash with a two minute video of some of the most amazing dunks you will ever see, including a 360 through the legs dunk at the 2011 Final Four NCAA slam dunk contest that had never been performed in a competition.

Jacob did not play for a basketball power and will never be an NBA lottery pick. He was a five-foot-ten-inch guard at little Division III Illinois College. I take pride in knowing itty bitty basketball schools, but I had never heard of that school. He showed up at the Denny's Slam Dunk Contest in Houston to compete against the high profile Division I players. Jacob was the shortest player in the competition. It came down to a dunk-off between Jacob and a player from UNC–Asheville. Jacob threw down a 360 dunk after catching a pass off the side of the backboard, and he stuck the landing. Jacob won the title to the astonishment of the capacity crowd.

Jacob was interviewed before his last dunk and was asked if he had used all of his good dunks or if he had any surprises left. His expression alone told you that he indeed had something special saved up. Kansas State All Big 12 guard Jacob Pullen said he didn't believe what he saw in the YouTube video could be real, but after seeing Jacob first hand in Houston, he became a believer.

One blog headline read, "5'10" White Kid Wins NCAA Slam Dunk Contest" after Jacob's performance. When I refereed Division III games, those white guards had trouble touching the rim. But Jacob is different. He is physically fit with incredible gymnastics ability as demonstrated by his cartwheel dunk and the way that he landed after his dunks. Jacob developed a phenomenal fifty-inch vertical leap through physical training and an edge gained from his research of explosive muscle twitches. He became a certified personal trainer at Illinois College.

Two thousand years ago, another astounding headline would have read, "Dead Lazarus Walks out of the Tomb." Jesus had already performed countless miracles such as healing the lame, restoring sight to the blind, turning water to wine, and feeding the five thousand with two loaves and five fishes. "So Jesus, have you used up all of your miracles, or do you have anything special saved up?" He indeed had saved one of his best for last just a few days before he would be falsely accused, severely beaten, and crucified.

Lazarus had been dead for four days. To prove a point, Jesus delayed his trip to Bethany for two days, which got everybody's attention, including the Jews, Martha, Mary, and his disciples. Jesus prayed and shouted, "Lazarus, come forth!" Lazarus came walking out of the tomb in his grave clothes. As Reverend T. D. Jakes once said, he was loosed!

Jesus used Lazarus to show his disciples what would happen to him after Calvary. At first the Jews couldn't believe it, but after they saw it, many believed that Jesus was indeed the Son of God and the Messiah. One of the greatest miracles had happened, and that miracle would be eclipsed when God brought Jesus out of the grave to walk among men again.

Jesus Christ is the same yesterday, today, and forever. Jesus proclaimed that he and his Father are one. God and Jesus are still in the miracle business just like they were when Jesus walked the earth. We continue to be encouraged by the miracles of healing that still occur and never doubt that God is in complete control.

Prayer: Dear Jesus, the miracles that you performed to help convince the people of Israel that you were indeed the Messiah were truly awesome. Thank you for the miracles that you perform today and will perform in the future because you never change. Thank you, Jesus, my Savior and my Lord. In your holy name. Amen.

BK84
TAKE THE JORTS 30/30
CHALLENGE

1 Corinthians 6:19–20

Or do you not know that your body is the temple of the
Holy Spirit who is in you, whom you have from God, and
you are not your own? For you were bought at a price;
therefore glorify God in your body and in your spirit, which
are God's.

One of the great personal interest stories from the 2010–2011
college basketball season was Josh Harrellson from the University
of Kentucky. In 2009, UK's former coach made him ride back
from Nashville in the equipment van after a poor performance,
and Josh averaged only two minutes of playing time per game. For
the 2010–2011 season, he was clearly plan B after the Cats signed
a future NBA lottery pick, Enes Kanter, from Turkey to replace
NBA first-rounder Demarcus Cousins. But despite the incessant
pleas of "Free Enes" from the Big Blue Nation, the NCAA declared Kanter permanently ineligible for receiving excessive com-
pensation for expenses from his Turkish pro team. Kentucky was
forced to go with the unheralded, unproven Harrellson as the big
man starter.

During preseason practice Harrellson, who was apparently irritated that he was not getting enough credit, expressed criticism about it in a tweet. Coach John Calipari stopped his tweeting and further disciplined Josh by running him on the treadmill for thirty minutes before every practice for thirty days. After this extensive conditioning, Harrellson could now play thirty to thirty-five minutes per game. UK needed those extra minutes from Josh because of a very thin bench.

Josh's turning point came when he had twenty-three points and fourteen rebounds in a win over archrival Louisville. Despite a midseason lull, Harrellson finished strong in the SEC tournament and landed a berth on the SEC All-Tournament team. Josh kept UK in the NCAA tournament with stellar first-half performances against Princeton and West Virginia. He played Ohio State's magnificent freshman Sullinger and North Carolina's talented Zeller to virtual draws, helping Kentucky advance to the Final Four.

The six-foot ten-inch Harrellson became a UK fan favorite. Affectionately known as Jorts because of his preference for jean shorts, Harrellson became a role model for every coach to encourage players who have underachieved or have not reached their potential. Jorts went from no future in pro basketball prior to the season to a future in a European league by midseason to a very likely future in the NBA. This opportunity was primarily made possible by the extra thirty minutes of running, which toughened Josh physically and mentally.

Josh was asked this question by ESPN's Scott Van Pelt and Ryan Russillo. "If I would have told you before the season, given you were behind most of the competition you're playing against in terms of NBA status that this is how your year would have turned out, what would you have thought?"

Josh answered, "I would have been in disbelief. I would have never believed it, but it's great what God does and all the situations he's put me in. You know, I'm thankful for it. I've made the most of everything he has given me."

I heard a striking message from a human energy expert, who explained the importance of balancing our spiritual, emotional, mental, and physical life components. A self-profile revealed that my neglect of physical training and bad eating habits cost me much-needed energy. The apostle Paul explained to the Corinthians that the human body is a temple of the Holy Spirit. We need to feed our temples the proper food, the proper exercise, and the proper messages. Christ paid the price for us, and it is our duty to honor and glorify God spiritually and physically each day. I committed to spend thirty additional minutes per day over the next thirty days in a combination of spiritual and physical training. It could be additional time in the morning reading the Bible, prayer, and meditation. Tomorrow, it could be pounding the pavement in my neighborhood. I hope the lifestyle change will improve my energy to help me fulfill my duties to God, my family, and my employer.

Who knows? As Josh saw a new door opened for him in the NBA, we could even see new doors opened. Take the "Jorts 30/30 challenge" with me and let's grow spiritually and physically.

Update: Josh Harrellson was drafted in the second round by the New York Knicks and played for the Knicks and the Miami Heat.

Prayer: Most gracious and giving God, thank you for the blessings that you give me each day, which includes the energy that I receive through proper nutrition, rest, and exercise. May I find a way to funnel new energy to maintain my life balance and help the kingdom flourish. Thank you for Jesus, who made our salvation possible on the cross. In Jesus's perfect and holy name. Amen.

BK85
THE STRONGEST
FORM OF FLATTERY

Ephesians 5:1–2, Galatians 5:22–23

Therefore be imitators of God as dear children. And walk in love, as Christ also has loved us and given himself for us, an offering and a sacrifice to God for a sweet-smelling aroma.

Ephesians 5:1–2

It's long been said that imitation is the most sincere form of flattery. When I was in college, I became enamored with "Pistol Pete" Maravich. When Pete was going well, I was up. When Pete had a bad game, I was down. When I was at the University of Georgia, my idolatry grew, and I began to imitate Pistol Pete. I grew my hair longer like Pete's; this was the 1970s when long hair was popular among young people. During his first year with the Jazz, Pete grew a long goatee, so I tried. For six weeks, I let my goatee and scruffy moustache grow. I went home for spring break, opened the door, and shocked my mother as her All-American son looked, well, less than All-American!

On the basketball court, I would throw my no-look passes, dribble behind my back, and put plenty of spin on my over-the-head shots off the glass. I would show no emotion in my game, not even the night that I threw in a fifty-five-foot underhanded rainbow. No, I had to be cool like Pete. I would shoot the same pull-up jumper and try to "take over games" in Stegeman Hall, just the way Pete did in the fourth quarter of NBA games. I wore the same brand of adidas Superstars that Pistol wore. I bought my Jazz number 7 jersey when I was in graduate school that I wore to the NCAA finals in Atlanta. Yes, imitation is the strongest form of flattery. Or is it? My idolatry was sinful in God's eyes because I put Pete and sports and many other things ahead of my relationship with Christ and others. My whole world and existence was built around sports, and I immersed myself in games. As Dr. Dennis Kinlaw points out in *This Day with the Master* (April 27), the Bible teaches us in Ephesians that the imitation of *Christ-like* qualities is where we need to be. We could never imitate Christ such as performing the miracles or walking on water. But we can display the fruit of the Spirit, which is described in Galatians 5:22–23 as "love, joy, peace, patience, kindness, goodness, faithfulness, gentleness, and self-control."

Soon after I watched Pete's testimony and was saved, I came to realize that I was imitating Pete again. But this time, it was in a positive way. I became interested in what other people were doing, and God's love penetrated and stilled my soul the same way it did Pete's during the last five years of his life. You could say that we were both trying to imitate Christ, the one who deserves all of the glory, honor, and praise that we can heap upon him and his most Holy Father.

Prayer: Most holy and omnipotent God, please forgive my sins, even the ones that I am not even aware of, so that I can imitate your Son and share the sweet-smelling aroma worthy of a child of God to everyone that I meet. In Jesus's name. Amen.

BK86
HAVING MERCY ON AN OPPONENT

1 Samuel 24

Now it happened afterward that David's heart troubled him because he had cut Saul's robe.

1 Samuel 24:5

My dad coached high school basketball for twenty-nine seasons. He won over eight hundred games, and he was first and foremost a gentleman. Dad never believed in taking advantage of a weaker opponent and running up the score on anyone. He recalled the time when a coach beat him 96–49. His comment was, "Every dog has his day." Years later, Dad upset the same coach in a region tournament and kept him from going to state. The rout earlier in his career had given Dad extra incentive to coach his team to a win if and when he should ever meet that coach again.

As Christians, we are supposed to show mercy in a world that says step on their necks and stomp the other team as bad as you can. I have always respected Coach Mark Richt of the Georgia Bulldogs. When Mark had some of his best teams, his stopping point seemed to be forty-five points. Mark would substitute his second string and third string into the game to keep the margin down, even though more points would have helped Georgia in the polls.

David also had an opportunity to step on the neck of Saul, the king of Israel, when he clearly had Saul at a disadvantage. David and his men were hiding in a cave when Saul entered to relieve himself. David could have killed Saul without any resistance, but he ordered his men not to attack. However, he cut the hem of Saul's garment and showed it to Saul later to prove that he did not take advantage of the opportunity that he had to kill him.

Let's emulate these examples of Coach Farr, Coach Richt, and King David and show mercy to someone else.

Prayer: Father God, restrain me from running up the score on someone who unfairly took advantage of me. It's just not what Jesus would do, so neither should I. Help me be like Jesus whether I am ahead or behind in the score. In the name of Jesus. Amen.

BK87
SWEET TALKERS

Jude

These are sensual persons, who cause divisions, not having
the Spirit.

Jude 19

My Friday morning Bible study group searched for a filler topic
until we began our next study. We decided to read the book of Jude.
One of the fellows wondered why Jude, as obscure as it is with
only one chapter and twenty-five verses, was even included in the
Bible. We discovered that Jude provided excellent instruction to
those within the church to watch for unbelievers and hypocrites
invading the church, and that we are to be on guard at all times.

An episode that happened at our Mt. Zion basketball ministry
brought home the teachings of Jude for me. One of my cardinal
rules was to observe how any new coach behaved for one season.
This grace period ensured that the coach performed adequately
as an assistant before being trusted with his or her own team
the following year. Our basketball ministry emphasizes equal
participation and good sportsmanship from coaches, players, and
spectators. We stress having fun in a competitive environment,
and our coaches should never place excessive pressure on the kids
to win. I messed up when I allowed two new coaches to co-coach
one of our middle school teams. I met them at registration, and

they were both experienced coaches who talked a good game and seemed to support our philosophy. I needed one more coach, and frankly, they told me what I wanted to hear.

I was at home the first Saturday afternoon of the season following my morning games when I received a phone call from John Ivors, our late referee emeritus. These two coaches turned out to be big-time complainers who received technical fouls during the game and cornered John after the game.

I had a tremendous predicament because half the boys on the team were friends of these coaches. If I let these coaches go, their friends would leave, and I had no other parents who could take over a remnant of a team. I chose to refund the registration fees to the coaches and players and spread the remaining boys on the team across the other three teams. This reshuffling required me to make between fifty and sixty phone calls and forced me to create a brand new schedule for this league.

If only I had followed the teachings of Jude, which warns leaders of the church how "certain men have crept in unnoticed... who turn the grace of our God into lewdness" (Jude 4). Jude further describes men who are "grumblers, complainers, walking according to their own lusts; and they mouth great flattering words, flattering people to gain advantage" (Jude 16). "These are sensual people, who cause divisions, not having the Spirit" (Jude 19).

Certainly, these two men were sweet talkers driven by their selfish ways and caused great division in our ministry that season; recalling this incident made Jude come alive for me. I guess Jude does belong in the Bible!

Prayer: Father God, thank you for the gift of wisdom and discernment that you give us. May we constantly be on guard for those who would act in such a way as to cause disruption in our ministries. Give us the courage and fortitude to deal with them firmly and decisively. In Jesus's name. Amen.

BK88
HEED THE ALERT

Ezekiel 12

And the word of the Lord came to me.

Ezekiel 12:1

I participated in a dozen referee camps as I aspired to climb the ladder of major college basketball officiating in the SEC or ACC. At these camps, the veteran officials taught us the nuances of the game and how to run our games as smoothly as possible. One adage that I recall was how to handle three seconds in the lane. Often, offensive post players will attempt to gain an advantage by staying in the three-second lane too long. You are taught to try to talk a player out of the lane, but you can't talk and talk and talk. At some point, you must blow the whistle. Otherwise, the player never suffers the consequence and will continue to "pitch a tent" in the lane. Veteran official Joe Forte taught our high school referees his philosophy, "Talk then blow." Tell the player once, which is the warning, and the next time that he camps out in the paint, blow the whistle and call three seconds. The other players see the consequence of the infraction and adapt by getting in and out of the lane appropriately for the remainder of the game.

God is very patient. He sent Major Prophets such as Isaiah, Jeremiah and Ezekiel and Minor Prophets such as Hosea, Micah, and Zechariah to tell the people of Israel to repent and change their evil ways. You would think they would have gotten it after learning about the disasters that previous generations went through. God didn't just talk. Through the prophets, he warned the people of what would happen, and when they failed to comply, he blew the whistle and doled out the consequences.

By hearing and obeying God's quiet voice, daily prayer, Bible reading and Bible study, and following the guidance of the Holy Spirit, we can heed the warnings that we are going down the wrong road. We can change our ways before we get whistled and suffer drastic consequences for our actions.

Prayer: Father God, you demonstrated your mercy to the people of Israel through the prophets who warned the people to change their evil ways before they suffered the consequences of their actions. Help me to take action the first time you point out to me that I need to change my ways before I suffer dire consequences. In Jesus's name. Amen.

BK89
GERT, WHO IS GRACE?

Ephesians 2:8–9

It is the gift of God. Not because of works, lest any man should boast.

Ephesians 2:9

Becca and I have very dear friends, who are family to us, in Glendale, Kentucky, named Mike and Sharon Bell. Mike has served over forty years as pastor of Becca's childhood church, Glendale Christian Church. He married us in 1981, and he married Allison and Kevin in 2012. Mike and Sharon have two beautiful granddaughters, Sam and Caehla, who are both accomplished athletes. Sam and Caehla affectionately call Sharon "Gert" and Mike "MoHo," which is short for Most Holy Reverend. Don't you love a pastor and a pastor's wife with a sense of humor?

When Sam was twelve, she participated in a week-long summer youth retreat in Campbellsville. On Wednesday night, she sent Sharon a text message. Caehla, who was eight, said, "Gert, who sent you a text?" Sharon said, "Sam did. She texted me, 'I was saved tonight.'" Caehla asked, "What do you mean, she was saved?" Sharon replied, "Well, Sam was saved by grace!" With all the innocence of youth, Caehla replied, "Gert, who is grace?"

That was a great question. Caehla didn't understand so she asked. Who is grace, or what is grace? Some girls are named Grace.

Sometimes, people say grace, or the blessing, before meals. So what is grace? Grace is God's unmerited favor that is available to each of us, no matter how badly you or I may have sinned against him. God loves you so much, and there are never any strings attached to receive his love. Grace is a free gift of his unending love, and you can never do enough good deeds to earn grace.

You've heard of mercy, and that God is a merciful God. Here is the difference between mercy and grace that Dr. Charles Stanley once explained. Mercy is *not* getting what you deserve. Grace is getting what you *don't* deserve.

Mercy is when God could punish you for your sin, but he is a forgiving God and often chooses not to discipline you fully for wrongdoing. Grace occurs when someone takes the discipline for you.

I gained the following understanding of mercy and grace from an illustration by John Wooden and Jay Carty in their book, *Coach Wooden: One-on-One*. Suppose you are on a basketball team and you break a team rule. The punishment for violating the rule is twenty suicides or gut drills. Sprint to the foul line and back, sprint to half court and back, sprint to the far foul line and back, and sprint to the other baseline and back. Mercy is after you have run ten gut drills, your coach says, "Okay, you don't have to run the last ten." Grace is after you have run ten gut drills, your coach says, "Sit down. I'll run the last ten for you."

Jesus Christ ran our gut drills on the cross! He took the punishment for our wrongdoing and paid the penalty for our sins. We didn't do anything to deserve his sacrifice. He died while we were still sinners. But God loves us so much that he allowed his only Son to be tortured and abused. Then Christ hung for six hours in excruciating pain on a cross with railroad-type spikes driven through his hands and feet. God could not look upon the sin that Jesus represented, so he turned the skies black. Jesus died for you so that one day you could choose to receive God's free gift of grace which you cannot earn.

Sam repented of her sins and accepted God's free gift of grace. God immediately granted her eternal life with him and Jesus now and in heaven, and the name "Samantha Bell" was written in The Book of Life. Hopefully, you have made or will make that same commitment if you now understand what grace really means.

Prayer: Father God, you are our loving, just, and merciful God, who loved us so much that you sent your Son from heaven to earth to pay the penalty for our sins. Thank you for Jesus covering us with his precious blood at Calvary. In Jesus's name. Amen.

BK90
A HELPING HAND

Matthew 25:34–46

When you refused to help the least of these my brothers and sisters, you were refusing to help me.

Matthew 25:45

I spoke to some girls at a summer basketball camp in Athens about "Pistol Pete" Maravich. After my talk my friend Taylor, who had invited me, and I were eating our lunches as we sat against the gym wall. He paused and said, "Look at that girl sitting by herself down there." Sure enough, there were about thirty-five girls chatting animatedly, but one girl sat by herself, obviously downcast and staring across the gym.

I said, "That was really good of you to notice her. I didn't even see her sitting down there. Why did you notice and I didn't?" Taylor said, "I've been there [like that kid]." To his credit, he called over to the coach, who sent two girls to talk to her. Within a few minutes, she sat in the middle of the girls, doing just fine.

The episode reminded me of a story shared by my friend Sherri at a lay speaking class. Sherri, a children's education leader at a local church, participated in a training class about caring and compassion with many lay people and church leaders. There were four tables at lunch. One table had a great spread of food with silverware. Two other tables had box lunches. The people at the fourth table had no food, and they sat uncomfortably while the others enjoyed their food.

Someone finally spoke up and asked why the fourth table didn't have any food. That revelation was the purpose of the training. It had been twenty-two minutes before a believer spoke up. Sherri shared that when the same experiment was attempted with a roomful of kids, it was only three minutes before one of the kids spoke up.

What can we learn from our kids? We are to have our eyes open for those who are hurting, and take the initiative to remove the hurt. Perhaps we need to see with the eyes of a child. Jesus made it clear that he hurts when we don't help others in need.

Prayer: O, God, when people near me are in need, may I hear them with your ears, see them with your eyes, and demonstrate caring and compassion. In Jesus's name. Amen.

BK91
HOW DO I KNOW
THAT GOD EXISTS?

Romans 1:20, 2 Corinthians 5:7, Psalm 139:14

For we walk by faith, not by sight.

2 Corinthians 5:7

I asked our six and seven year olds these questions at Hoops2Heaven before explaining to them about our loving God whom we cannot see. How do you know that a builder made this gym? What proof do you have? You didn't see anyone lay these blocks to build the walls, or lay this floor, or paint the lines, or hang these lights. Why do you believe that someone built this gym intentionally and this isn't just some random occurrence that happened?

How do you know that God made you? The Bible says that you are fearfully and wonderfully made (Psalm 139:14). A commentary in *The Way of the Master Bible* tells us that your eyeball has 137 million tiny light cells. That's no accident!

Think about the world and universe that we live in. How do you know that God made it? How do you know that there is a God? A vast and complex universe with such intricate detail didn't just happen. Consider how the earth rotates once every twenty-four hours, and how the sun rises and sets, and how the high and low tides of the ocean can be predicted to the minute.

When my family was on spring vacation in Florida, we watched the sunset from the beach. We watched until the last sliver of orange dropped below the horizon. Sure enough it disappeared at 7:37 the first night, 7:38 the second night, and 7:39 the third night. Perfectly on time as predicted by the calendar. Consider the water cycle, how water evaporates and leaves the earth, then returns as rain. Think of the majestic mountains *under the sea*! Genesis reveals that during the big flood the water covered the mountains. There are mountains over a mile high under the ocean! The Bible makes it clear that everything in the world was made by God. The reason that we know God exists is because we have *faith*. Even when we can't prove it, we know that it is so because *the Bible says so*.

Prayer: Dear God, thank you for the faith you give me, as small as a mustard seed sometimes, that I can still believe in what cannot be seen. Even though I cannot see you, I know that people saw Jesus two thousand years ago and believed. Help me daily to walk by faith, not by sight. Greater are my blessings when I can't see you and Jesus, but still I believe. In Jesus's holy name. Amen.

BK92
MISGUIDED AMBITION

Jeremiah 29:11

I know the plans that I have for you, declares the Lord, plans for welfare and not for harm, to give you a future and a hope. (NASB)

My consistent dream for twenty years was to become an SEC men's basketball official. But before the SEC, there would be hundreds of car rides to obscure small colleges. Plenty of rushing out of work to beat the traffic to get to gyms on time then late night journeys back home from Valdosta, Savannah, Birmingham and plenty of points in between!

I refereed at Francis Marion College in Florence, South Carolina, on a Monday night. In the women's game a player was injured and the game went into overtime, so the men's game started just before nine o'clock. I remember sitting in a Wendy's drive-thru in Florence at 11:30 p.m., wondering how I could possibly get back to Atlanta that night.

I arrived in Madison, Georgia, at 3:30 a.m. and wearily pulled into a Days Inn to catch two hours of sleep before going to work. That evening, I had a game at Truett McConnell College in Cleveland, Georgia. I was in no frame of mind to referee. I had a terrible game, and called technical fouls on a coach and a player out of frustration.

You could categorize this part of my officiating odyssey as "misguided ambition." My wife Becca—who was so supportive while I chased my dream—and my daughters were thrilled to have me home when I eventually gave up college officiating in 1998.

In 2011, I saw my buddy Steve referee a state tournament game at Wheeler High School in Marietta. He and I refereed fifty games together when I chased my dream, and it was great catching up with him. Steve told me that he would drive back and forth from his home in Cleveland to Statesboro the following two nights.

I immediately flashed back to the car trips that had led to nowhere. I thanked God for my ministry with the kids in the gym and for my stable job. If I had made the SEC, who knows what would have happened with my marriage and my job. God always knows what is best for us, and he knows when misguided ambition overtakes us. If you are currently running a rat race like I was, ask God if those activities are really what he wants you doing.

Prayer: Dear Father God, thank you for forgiving me for all of the stuff I've done that was driven by misguided ambition. Surely you cringed when you saw the broad road that I was on. I am so grateful that you are the God of second, third, fourth, and one hundredth chances. I am filled with gratitude that you never gave up on me. In the name of Jesus. Amen.

BK93
ANTI-ESTABLISHMENT

Matthew 5:1–12

Blessed are the pure in heart, for they shall see God.

Matthew 5:7

Sports Illustrated ran an awesome two-page photo of Pete Maravich. The photo was taken when LSU played at Tulane in late 1968 when America was truly in a time of great upheaval and transition. When you observe the players on the court, every player has on the same white socks except Pete, whose socks are gray and floppy. Every player has a conservative short haircut, but Pete's mop top style is a prelude that longer hair would soon become the norm among men.

Basketball players during the 1960s used the same basic fundamentals, but Pete sprinkled in plenty of behind-the-back dribbles and between-the-legs passes. Pete's flamboyant style of play, which was nicknamed *Showtime*, was the sign of things to come. Pete and his dad and coach, Press, refused to conform to the norm as they ushered in a new era that would transform the basketball establishment.

Jesus was anti-establishment too. He didn't follow the Pharisees' examples of praying out loud in public and making sure everybody knew how much money you were giving to the temple.

Jesus treated everyone fairly regardless of his or her heritage. Jesus preached that the poor, the oppressed, and women had just as much right to the kingdom of God as anyone else.

Prayer: Dear Lord, thank you for the vision and follow through of Christians who are building churches that don't resemble traditional churches. I pray that these new churches will demonstrate to people that Jesus was not simply about conformity, but he was completely about love, inclusion, forgiveness, and grace. In Jesus's name. Amen.

BK94
KEVIN DURANT

2 Timothy 3:16–17

All Scripture is given by inspiration of God, and is profitable for doctrine, for reproof, for correction, for instruction in righteousness, that the man of God may be complete, thoroughly equipped for every good work.

Kevin Durant was a lottery pick of the Oklahoma City Thunder and led the NBA in scoring during his first two seasons. Durant put together a number of impressive streaks such as consecutive games over thirty points, consecutive games with at least one three-point field goal, consecutive field goals made, and consecutive free throws made.

Perhaps his most impressive streak came in March 2011 after he attended a chapel meeting before a game in Memphis. The Memphis team chaplain challenged those present to read the Bible daily. Durant started a streak of reading his Bible daily and was up to forty-four consecutive days when he was seen at a press conference with his music player, headphones, and his Bible. He explained the challenge that he had accepted to the media.

"I'm keeping strong at it, just trying to make my walk with faith a little better. That's making me a better person, opening my eyes to things, and I'm also maturing as a person. I'm just trying to grow."

After receiving the online article from my coach friend Rick Johnson, I shared Durant's story with the high school boys at open gym. I had talked to them about reading the Bible the previous two Thursday nights. I said, "I cannot make it [the gospel] any more relevant for you than telling you that [Kevin Durant], the NBA's leading scorer, who has it all in front of him, saw a way to improve his walk and believes it is important to be in the Word [daily]."

How about you? Is it time to put a winning streak together? Just a few minutes in the morning will put you on the way to a more powerful relationship with Christ and can help your relationships at home, at school, and at work.

Prayer: Dear Father God, may Kevin Durant continue to read his Bible, grow in Christ, and be a mighty witness wherever NBA games are shown around the world. Please use him to bring many people to know Jesus. In Jesus's name. Amen.

BK95
OVERCALLING, UNDERCALLING, JUST RIGHT!

Philippians 1:1–6

Being confident of this very thing, that He who has begun a good work in you will complete until the day of Jesus Christ.

Philippians 1:6

For most beginner basketball officials, there are three stages in an official's development. In the first stage, you are afraid to blow the whistle. You're scared that you're going to be wrong when you're actually being wrong every time you allow a foul or violation to go unpunished. That's undercalling. Second, after you gain some confidence, blowing the whistle and the attention that comes with it starts feeling good to you. Now you're blowing the whistle so much that you are interfering with the flow and enjoyment of the game. That's overcalling. Third, when you are able to scale back your whistle-blowing and make your calls based on advantage or disadvantage, you start to get it right. Finding the happy medium is the third and final stage of becoming an experienced official.

We undercall for God when we are unbelievers and are of no help to the kingdom. We aren't doing anything that God made us for that would help grow his kingdom. As baby Christians, we overcall by thinking we are God's gifts to the world, possibly turning some people away from the Lord, or making your family a little crazy and frustrated as I did! In the overcalling stage, we run ahead of God and chase our ideas without properly validating them with God and other Christians. But thankfully, maturity and growth follow, and by heeding guidance from mature Christians, we finally get in step with God's plan and begin to get it just right (see Philippians 1:6).

Those three stages remind me of Goldilocks and the three bears—too cold, too hot, then just right!

Prayer: Most holy God, may I not be discouraged because I don't exactly know how to live this Christian life. I have faith that you will lead me in the way of obedience by reading your word and coming to you frequently in prayer. Thank you for the discernment that I do have and for your faith in me. In the holy name of my Savior. Amen.

BK96
GET A T.O. BABY!

2 Timothy 3:1–16

All Scripture is given by inspiration of God and is profitable for doctrine, for reproof, for correction.

2 Timothy 3:16 (KJV)

Dick Vitale is one of college basketball's most fervent spokespersons. I recall a beleaguered Bob Ley of ESPN about 10:30 p.m. one evening; he and Dickie V. had been on the air for ten straight hours covering the NCAA first round games. Ley was clearly out of gas, but Vitale was still running wide-open with his effusive praise of just about anyone who had made a basket.

Vitale has coined many sayings during his career, such as diaper dandies (promising freshmen), PTPers (prime-time players who are at their best in the big games), and "Get a T.O. [time-out] baby!" Vitale says get a time-out after the home team has punctuated an 11–0 run with a resounding dunk as the student section and entire arena go crazy! The visiting team needs to call a time-out in order to regroup.

Sometimes, we need to get a time-out when we have drifted off course from God's direction and guidance. He may even take us out of the action through discipline that is akin to a time-out. It's up to us to recognize his action, the reason for it, and to get back in sync with his plan. Oftentimes, it means admitting our actions were selfish and confessing that we've put ourselves ahead of him (again). Confess your mistakes, receive God's forgiveness, and get back in the action!

Prayer: Dear Holy Father, I didn't like time-out as a kid. I don't enjoy time-outs now, but I realize that I need one now and then for my own good, and for the benefit of those who live with me, work with me, or go to school with me. Thank you for your corrections which make me a stronger disciple. In the name of Jesus. Amen.

BK97
ACCUMULATED SINS

Psalm 19:12, Psalm 51:10, 1 John 1:9

If we confess our sins, He is faithful and just to forgive us our sins and to cleanse us from all unrighteousness.

1 John 1:9

Veteran official Hank Nichols shared this story with the referees at a Nationwide Basketball Referee summer camp. He was officiating a game at Syracuse University, and Coach Jim Boeheim was whining about calls that were going against him. Boeheim was chipping away, which means that he was nitpicking the various calls that Hank and his partner had made. After one too many chips, Hank blew his whistle and gave Boeheim a technical foul.

With his mouth agape, Boeheim threw both hands in the air, and said, "What did I do to deserve a *T*?" In his mind, the *T* was unwarranted because he had not done anything different than the other times that he complained.

Hank replied, "It was the accumulation of chips that earned you the *T*."

God cares about us deeply, and it hurts him each time we chip away with sin and draw further away from him. After one too many chips, he may send us a message through a family member, friend or circumstance that makes us sit up and pay attention.

In a sense, he calls us to stop repeating and to repent. Heed his call, earnestly repent, and live for him anew.

Prayer: Most gracious and just God, I am sure that I try your patience quite often. May I learn more rapidly from my sinful mistakes and cause you less angst. In the holy name of Jesus Christ. Amen.

BK98
SANDWICHED

Isaiah 58:8–12

For the Lord will go before you, and the God of Israel will be your rear guard.

Isaiah 58:8

Kareem Abdul-Jabbar ranks as the second most prolific scorer in the history of professional basketball with over forty-seven thousand points. His patented sky hook was a revolutionary invention because nobody could block the shot, which he seemed to flip down into the basket.

In college, when he was known as Lew Alcindor, he was double-teamed in the post on virtually every play in UCLA's half-court offense. One player fronted him to keep him from catching the ball, and the opposing center guarded him from the rear. He was figuratively sandwiched between two players.

Often, God sandwiches you in a layer of protection, and you probably don't even realize it. He's out front, knocking down barriers and making crooked paths straight for you before you turn the corner or even wake up for the day. You don't even know about the troubles he protects you from.

He also has your back, protecting you from the evil in the world that would love to bring you down. You're safe in God's loving embrace, sort of like the shelter of a cocoon. God protects his children whom he loves perfectly.

Prayer: Dear Lord, thank you for your awesome protection. I cannot comprehend the extent of your love and protection. I know that you love me so much that you will do whatever you can to protect me. Thank you for having my back and knocking down barriers to help me get where I am going. In the precious name of our Lord Jesus Christ. Amen.

BK99
THIRD MAN THROUGH

2 Timothy 3:16–17

All Scripture is given by inspiration of God and is profitable for doctrine, for reproof, for correction.

2 Timothy 3:16 (KJV)

Basketball officiating is all about getting the proper angles. When an official blows a call, it's usually because he had a bad angle. One of the most often missed calls is when the defender is directly between the official and the offensive player with the ball. The official is the third man in a straight line. That's bad news when you are officiating! You can't see if the defender blocked the ball cleanly or got a piece of the shooter's arm without seeing the play from an angle.

At the 2011 Final Four, Becca, Allison, Jillian, and I were sitting in what could be described as beyond nosebleed seats in section 640 in the corner of Reliant Stadium. During the first half with about six minutes remaining, a UConn player drove for the basket and appeared to run right over Josh Harrellson, the Kentucky center. But the call was a block! Now, I was about a thousand feet away as the crow flies, but I was so certain that the official was wrong. I leaped out of my seat and almost fell into the row in front of us! It was Josh's second foul, so Coach Calipari sat him for the duration of the half. UConn pulled away to a ten-point lead while he was on the bench.

When we returned home, I watched the replay on YouTube, and sure enough, the official who made the call was straight-lined (third man through). I am not saying that the play cost UK the one-point loss, but it didn't help!

Living daily without the word of God is like being the third man through. Without God's word to guide you, it's difficult to discern where you should be. When you blend into the secular world, you can't see Satan's wiles because you have lost your angle. Reading and studying God's word will give you better angles that will help you make the right decision much more often.

Prayer: Dear Lord, help me stay true to the Bible and read it daily so that I get the proper angles from your Word. In Jesus's name. Amen.

BK100
SHORT SHORTS

Philippians 2:9–11, Revelation 19:11–16

And He has on His robe and on His thigh a name written:
King of Kings and Lord of Lords

Revelation 19:16

Michael Jordan is given credit for changing the fashion of basketball shorts. In the mid-1980s basketball players still wore mid-thigh length basketball trunks, but Michael had Champion make his Chicago Bulls shorts four to six inches longer, almost down to his knees. The fad spread like wildfire. Virtually, every player at all levels of basketball, except old-school John Stockton, adopted the free-flowing look. Surely, we will all be with the Lord before basketball shorts revert back to 1980s length.

Because the basketball shorts are so long, it's easy for the manufacturers to put the entire school name or nicknames on the side of the shorts. In fact, you could probably put a short essay on some trunks that hang below the knee!

Did you know Jesus has a name written on his robe and even on his thigh? Sure enough, the book of Revelation reveals that when Jesus comes to save the world, he will have the following names written on his thigh: "King of Kings and Lord of Lords" (Revelation 19:16). God has given Jesus the name above all names. When Jesus returns, every knee will bow, and every tongue on earth, in heaven, or below the earth will declare that Jesus Christ is Lord (Philippians 2:9–11).

Prayer: Dear Lord, I long for the day when Christ returns in all of his glory to rule this earth. Help me look forward to and be prepared for his coming. In Jesus's name. Amen.

BK101
I CHOSE YOU

John 15:16, 1 John 4:19

You did not choose Me, but I chose you.

John 15:16

One of the most ballyhooed and publicized events of the sports year is the NBA draft in June at Madison Square Garden in New York City. NBA owners and general managers select players in the first and second rounds who will hopefully make a big difference in their teams for years to come.

An aspiring player undergoes a series of workouts in cities across the country prior to the draft. He strives to impress one team so favorably that he is not only drafted but is taken as a lottery pick.

The owners control the draft. The player has no choice whom he plays for. The player doesn't choose the team. The team chooses the player.

It's like that with you and God. God chose you. He chose you to be his child before you were born. You didn't do the choosing. Except you can now, because you can choose to be a Christ follower or you can choose to ignore him. In fact, it's your choice to play for the most amazing God, who loved you first and loves you so infinitely that you can't even get your arms around its vastness. He chose you because he wants to spend a lot of time with you, both here on earth through the Holy Spirit which lives inside each believer, and in heaven, when God will prepare a permanent and everlasting home for you.

Always remember that even when you are in a rut and no matter how selfishly you are acting, God still chose you, and he still thinks you are the greatest thing going. God made you to be great with him, not without him.

Prayer: Most high God, thank you for choosing me first and for your never-ending love and concern for my well-being. It's the greatest thing in the world that you want to know me personally. May I grow in my desire to know you better. In Christ's name. Amen.

BK102
ONE SHINING MOMENT

Revelation 1:14–17

His countenance was like the sun shining in its strength.

Revelation 1:16

The NCAA Men's basketball national champion is crowned on the first Monday night in April. After the championship game ends, fans across the country look forward to the highlight package which captures the drama, the excitement, the heartbreak, and the exhilaration of March Madness. The musical arrangement for the video is entitled *One Shining Moment* and was written by David Barrett Hodges. CBS analyst Jim Nantz called *One Shining Moment* the anthem of the NCAA tournament.

Thousands of college basketball players have dreamed of their one shining moment, memorizing the words and using the song as inspiration during the season to spur their team toward a shot at the national title. The apostle John had one shining moment that he never forgot. Exiled on the isle of Patmos, he had escaped a tortured death that befell the other disciples of Christ. In the first chapter of Revelation, John wrote that he suddenly came face to face with Jesus Christ. John wrote that "His eyes were like a flame of fire (1:14). His countenance was like the sun shining in its strength (1:16)." When John saw Jesus, he fell at his feet as if he were dead. But Jesus reassured John, "Do not be afraid. I am the First and the Last" (1:17).

John's completely awestruck reaction reminds me of *I Can Only Imagine* by MercyMe, which is basically about how you will react the first time that you encounter Jesus in heaven. I imagine that the joyous reaction is both thrilling and unique for every believer. The most important point is not how you will react when you see Jesus for the first time, but *if* you will have an opportunity to react. Do you know without a doubt today that you are positioned to experience your "one shining moment" when you get to meet Jesus face to face? Now is the perfect time to repent and place your trust in Christ.

Prayer: Holy Father, thank you for the day that I will experience my one shining moment when I see Jesus for the first time. You loved me so much that you sent Jesus to die for my sin, and you raised him from the grave. Thank you for the miracle of Jesus, your greatest gift of all. In the name of the One who saves us. Amen.

BK103
STAY LOYAL TO THE TEAM

Matthew 26:20–25, 26:47–50; 27:1–10

When evening had come, He sat down with the twelve. Now as they were eating, He said, 'Assuredly, I say to you, one of you will betray Me.'

Matthew 26:20–21

The University of Kentucky men's basketball team won its eighth national championship by defeating Kansas 67–59 as the Big Blue Nation celebrated in "Blue Orleans." The title was especially sweet for Coach John Calipari, who blended three extremely talented freshmen, two sophomores, and a savvy senior who came off the bench as the sixth man.

It was only the fourth national title in NCAA history that was won by a team with a freshman point guard. Kentucky's point guard was Marquis Teague from Indianapolis. Perhaps Marquis had the most difficult adjustment because he was a high-scoring high school McDonald's All-American. But the role that Coach Cal needed Marquis to play was completely opposite from his years in high school and AAU. Marquis had been the star. Now Cal needed him to distribute the basketball and take fewer shots. The transition was difficult. In an early season game against Kansas in Madison Square Garden, perhaps Marquis was anxious to show the nation what he could do. At halftime, Marquis had no points and six turnovers. In the second half, Marquis made five baskets and no turnovers. Cal benched Marquis frequently during the season when Marquis strayed from his responsibilities and tried to do too much by himself. Obviously, there was tremendous pressure on him under the bright lights of the Final Four.

Would Marquis revert to selfish play or demonstrate his commitment to the team? As he ate his pregame meal with the team and his coach, surely thoughts of the NBA entered his mind. This would be his last college game before entering the NBA draft. It was a night that the entire country would be watching. If he had a great game, he could push himself from a probable second round selection to a late first round selection. His coach had made it abundantly clear. Take care of the basketball, take smart shots, and lead the team.

Marquis had a choice. He could shoot for personal glory and betray his coach and teammates in the process, or he could give himself up for the team. Marquis wisely chose the latter, and his team blended together seamlessly. His stat line from the championship game was fourteen points, three assists and only two turnovers. He made five points in the last four minutes as Kentucky withstood a furious Kansas rally. His team stayed united and captured the crown!

There was a disciple named Judas who ate a pregame meal with eleven teammates (the disciples) and his coach (Jesus) before the biggest game of their lives. In the upper room, Judas chose to betray his teammates for selfish gain at the most crucial time. Jesus told his team that the one who dipped his bread in the gravy would betray them. Judas chose to betray Jesus for thirty pieces of silver by handing Jesus over to the Jewish mob, who helped the Roman centurions hang him from a cross within twelve hours. The members of the disciple team that Jesus coached for three years scattered during his time of need.

Each day, we have opportunities to stand strong for Christ and the body of Christ, the church. We also have temptations to follow our selfish desires and betray him, which makes a negative impact on the kingdom of God. Consider what your choices will be. Will you betray Jesus or stand strong for the kingdom?

Prayer: Father God, help me stay strong and united for my teams, especially my church and for Jesus Christ, who paid the penalty for my unfaithfulness. May I follow your will unwaveringly to make the biggest impact that I possibly can for your kingdom. In the name of the One who went to the cross for all mankind. Amen.

BK104
LIN, LIN, LIN? WIN, WIN, WIN!

Matthew 5:16, Colossians 1:27

Let your light so shine before men, that they may see your good works and glorify your Father in heaven.

Matthew 5:16

The 2011–2012 NBA season began as a totally forgettable one for the New York Knicks. After a lockout lasted more than five months, the season finally began on Christmas Day. Six weeks later, the Knicks languished with an 8–15 record, well back in the Eastern Division. Three starters were out of action, and things appeared to be getting worse by the day as hopes of making the playoffs began to fade.

Enter Jeremy Lin, an undrafted rookie out of that basketball powerhouse, Harvard University. Harvard? Jeremy, a six-foot three-inch guard, came out of the NBA D-League (Development League) for a ten-day trial with the Knicks. Jeremy had already been cut by two NBA teams, and perhaps this would be his last stop if this stint didn't work. Thanks to an injury to New York's point guard, Jeremy got his chance. And did he ever take advantage of it! He scored more points in his first five NBA games than any player since the 1974 season and led the Knicks to five straight wins. His sudden success in the Big Apple landed him superstar attention from the fans who were starving for any glimmer of hope.

Jeremy became an instant hero, and his press conferences were carried live by ESPN. Jeremy hit a three-pointer with one second left to beat Toronto for New York's sixth consecutive win and followed it up with thirteen assists as the Knicks made it seven in a row against Sacramento.

More importantly, Jeremy gave his fellow Asian-Americans reason to cheer by becoming the biggest success that ethnic group had ever experienced in basketball. He smashed stereotypes about the ability of Asian-Americans to compete at the highest level.

The coolest thing of all? He is a Christian who is as serious about growing in his faith as his ability to handle the double team. Jeremy once described for Intervarsity Sports how prayer, Bible study, and his small group at Harvard had shaped his faith. "First, I need to be in the word daily. I read and pray in the morning and at night. It helps me get off to a good start in the morning and at night I look back at what happened during the day. And it's really important to me to go to church, which is sometimes tough when I get back from road trips late on Saturday night, but I try to make it a priority to go every week. That helps me a lot. And I meet weekly for discipleship with Adrian Tam, my Intervarsity staff worker. Having small group once a week gives me a lot of encouragement and accountability. Even though I go to church, I don't really know many people there, but my real community is my small group."

During an interview after one of the wins, Jeremy described that the most fun for him had been seeing the team come together as a cohesive unit. His ability to score and pass the basketball was surpassed by his capability to help his teammates collectively elevate their games.

Whose "games" or lives are you elevating? If you are only trying to elevate your life, you aren't helping people around you. In fact, you could be dragging them down. If you are living your life for Christ and letting your light shine (Matthew 5:16), you will disciple people around you and inspire them with the hope of Christ that is in you, the hope of glory (see Colossians 1:27). When you inspire others through your words, deeds, and actions in the name of Christ, that makes you a rising superstar in God's eyes.

Update: Jeremy Lin signed a multiyear contract with the Houston Rockets in 2012.

Prayer: Father God, thank you for Jeremy Lin, who not only gave the Knicks and the NBA a shot in the arm, but he gave millions of fans an example of how to be successful on the court and off the court for Christ. In Jesus's name. Amen.

BK105
THE GIVER OF ALL GOOD THINGS

Isaiah 64:4, 1 Corinthians 2:9, James 1:17

Every good and perfect gift is from above, and comes down from the Father of lights.

James 1:17

Ernie Johnson Jr. (E. J.) is the host of the popular *Inside the NBA* basketball series on Turner Network Television (TNT) featuring Charles Barkley, Shaquille O'Neal, and Kenny Smith. E. J. gave a marvelous sermon at Mt. Zion UMC on our Hoops2Heaven Sunday in 2012. After the 11:00 a.m. service, Ernie and I went to our gym for the season-ending Hoops2Heaven celebration for our players and their families. I enjoyed interviewing Ernie, and I asked him to tell the kids about Knicks sensation Jeremy Lin. Ernie shared some super words of encouragement, faith, and wisdom with the young boys and girls who surrounded us in front of our makeshift stage. I was especially appreciative that Ernie handed each player his or her trophy as he congratulated them.

Then came an awesome moment for young Chris, a twelve-year-old with a passion for basketball and a Christlike attitude on the floor and off. Chris is a big NBA fan, and his coach asked Ernie to pose with him for a picture. As they set up for the picture, Ernie looked down and noticed that Chris was wearing some rather large shoes.

Ernie teased, "You've got some big feet on you. What size shoe do you wear?" Chris answered, "14." Ernie said, "Stay here, I'll be right back."

Ernie walked out to his car. When he came back, he had a big shoe box in his hands. Ernie handed Chris a beautiful pair of size 14, black and red, Derrick Rose basketball shoes that are known as the d rose 2. Chris grinned from ear to ear!

Why was this such a cool moment? Chris's mom sent me an email that the day before she had told Chris that he could only wear his d rose 1 shoes one more time because he had worn them out! She wrote that Chris was so excited with his new basketball shoes that he would have slept in them if she had let him!

God is the giver of all good and perfect things. Chris will remember this moment forty years from now because the right shoes are a big, big deal to an aspiring basketball player. Sometimes God's gifts are material, and sometimes, they are spiritual. It is important that we learn to recognize all of God's gifts, not just the really cool ones that we never see coming. When we learn to recognize all that God does for us, we will grow in our appreciation and love for him.

Prayer: Father God, thank you for Ernie Johnson Jr.'s strong witness for Christ, and may you continue to bless him and his family richly. Thank you for using him to create a truly memorable moment in a deserving young man's life. In Jesus's name. Amen.

BK106
WINNING STATE FOR KATE!

Ecclesiastes 3:1, 4; Isaiah 55:8, 1 Corinthians 2:9,
James 1:17, 4:6

Eye has not seen, nor ear heard, nor have entered into the
heart of man, the things which God has prepared for those
who love him.

1 Corinthians 2:9

The St. Francis Lady Knights defeated Southwest Atlanta
Christian Academy 62–56 in overtime to win the 2013 Georgia
Class A Private School Girls Championship in Macon. Led by
head coach Alisha Kennedy, St. Francis was undersized with no
starter approaching six feet, while SACA had two starters who
topped out at six feet two inches. The Lady Knights immediately
fell behind 8–0 in the first ninety seconds and were down by ten
late in the third quarter before going on an 11–0 run. St. Francis's
hopes were bleak when they were down by four with twenty
seconds left in the game.

However, SACA traveled with the ball, and the Lady Knights
made two free throws. After a missed SACA free throw came the
biggest play of the game. Jade Davis, St. Francis's diminutive five-
foot four-inch guard, got the rebound amidst the tall trees, drove
the length of the floor, and took it hard to the basket. Closely
guarded by a SACA defender, she got hammered across her right

arm but powered a runner off the glass, and the ball banked in! It was an incredible shot under pressure! She missed her free throw, but her teammate Nettie Jones made a superb defensive play on the other end to force overtime. In the extra period, St. Francis shut down SACA's offense, and Candice Williams made the last of her eight-for-eight clutch free throws to ice the game.

St. Francis took an improbable ride to the championship game. During the preseason, Nigia Greene, the best all-around player and University of Miami signee, was making unsatisfactory progress from a knee injury. I was at the North Fulton Physical Therapy clinic when St. Francis assistant coach A.G. Crockett, my great friend and golf buddy, brought her to see Dr. Young. Nigia battled through her therapy sessions and finally played her first game several weeks before the state championship game, which was only her eighth game of the season. Without Nigia receiving the physical therapy that she needed, St. Francis would have had very little chance against SACA.

In November, Coach Crockett was asked to come to a team meeting before school started. To A.G.'s complete surprise, Nigia and the other seniors unveiled the team's new shoes. On the tongues of the shoes, the girls placed the name "Kate." A.G. was deeply moved when the girls told him that they were dedicating the season to Kate, A.G. and Gayley's daughter and sister of John. Three months earlier, Kate, age twenty-four, went to be with the Lord after an incredibly gutsy and courageous eighteen-month battle with cancer. The girls also trimmed the black shoes in lime green, the color that honors cancer patients.

During the previous seven months, there had been many struggles for Kate's parents to make it through each day. The state tournament run had been a pleasant distraction for Coach Crockett that brought him great pleasure. After a long season of immense sorrow, indeed it was time for something to celebrate! "To everything there is a season, a time for every purpose under heaven" (Ecclesiastes 3:1). "A time to weep, and a time to laugh, a time to mourn, and a time to dance" (Ecclesiastes 3:4).

After the final horn sounded, the coaches hugged each other, the girls celebrated at midcourt, and the St. Francis fans cheered! Then a very special thing happened. Perhaps realizing how much the victory meant to Coach Crockett, one of the players walked over to him, put her head on his shoulder, and gave him a gentle hug. I am certain that the girls recognized his grace, courage, humility, and love for them throughout the season. James 4:6 makes it clear that "he gives more grace…to the humble." The team's love and support must have been very heartwarming to A.G., who pointed in acknowledgment to his family and close friends behind the St. Francis bench. I pray that "Coach" sensed God's deep and abiding love washing over him during these special moments.

It was an incredible game with an amazing conclusion in regulation. Thinking of Kate after SACA turned it over with twenty seconds to play in regulation and St. Francis down by four, I turned to my friend Jeff and said, "They can still win this." Did God orchestrate the last twenty seconds of regulation? There will be various opinions, but certainly, he knew the outcome. Kate played high school basketball before completing her English degree at UNC and landing her dream job with a Manhattan publisher. Kate and A.G. often shared their love for basketball and especially the UNC Tar Heels. Throughout the championship run, A.G. would have enjoyed discussing the games with Kate because she would have totally been into the team and gotten it completely. But one glorious day, they will have all the time they will ever need to remember the day in Macon that St. Francis won state for Kate.

Prayer: Father God, thank you for the unexpected gifts that you give us when we really need them. Bless the girls who recognized how much it would mean to the family to dedicate the season to Kate. Please continue to strengthen and bless this wonderful family with your presence and love. In Jesus's name. Amen.

BK107
CELEBRATION OF A LIFETIME

One day at a time, sweet Jesus.

—*One Day at a Time*, Cristy Lane, 1974

At 1:15 a.m. on February 10, 2013, I heard Dad's walker scrape across the tile floor in his bathroom. I hopped out of bed and stood at his bedroom door to make sure he didn't stumble going back to bed. He sensed my presence and asked me to turn on the light. I told him that it was Sunday, February 10, and I said, "Happy one-hundredth birthday!" He exclaimed, "I'm a hundred years old!" He went back to bed, and I couldn't get back to sleep because I was so excited for him!

At the nine o'clock service at Cadwell-Rentz UMC, there were nineteen family members representing four generations. My niece, April, beautifully sang *One Day at a Time*, my dad's favorite song that he has mentioned frequently for the past several months. He often said, "Have you ever heard that song, *One Day at a Time?*" I shared a devotion about his bountiful tomato harvests, and Pastor Paulk concluded his sermon by recognizing Dad for the bountiful harvests that he has produced as a faithful servant, teacher, coach, father, and tomato grower for the community!

Over 200 people dropped by his home that afternoon to celebrate his birthday. Dad was stylish in his navy suit with a tiny pinstripe. He thoroughly enjoyed chatting and reminiscing with his friends and former students. Ouida, the star of his 1951 Girls State Championship team at Cedar Grove, was one of the first to congratulate him. I had never met this legendary player who I heard about all my life, and I hugged her with glee. A.D., the center on the 1952 Cedar Grove boys team, introduced himself, and Coach Farr immediately reminded him of a humorous hunting story during A.D.'s high school days.

Dad received more than eighty cards from as far away as California and New Jersey. Many wrote him notes about how he had helped shape their lives. A former student told him that she never understood math until he explained it to her. Another former student, who obviously had serious health issues, kept coming back to sit by Dad. The following day, Dad repeatedly said, "It was quite a day, wasn't it?"

It was an amazing day, not like any that I had ever experienced. Four days later, it was so big that I was still not able to wrap my arms around it. It was "God-size" big. It was beyond the joy of a family reunion on a beautiful day with temperatures in the mid-60s. Friends spilled out of the house into the front yard to visit and reminisce. There was nothing about the day that we would have changed.

It was an incredible blessing and truly a slice of heaven for my dad, the newest centenarian, to enjoy such a day in good health that so few will ever experience. It was a huge blessing for his three children and the family members who were present for the big occasion.

I searched the scriptures to help me express the joy that surrounded us that Sunday. I found this verse, which is Psalm 16:11, "You will show me the path of life; In your presence is fullness of joy; at your right hand are pleasures evermore." And of course Psalm 118:24, "This is the day that the Lord has made. Let us rejoice and be glad in it." We did indeed rejoice!

Prayer: Holy Father God, thank you for the legacy of Coach Farr, your child who is now in his second century. I thank you for each new morning that my dad gets to enjoy until he joins you one day. Until then, thank you for one day at a time. In sweet Jesus's name. Amen.

VERSES BY BOOK

2:9		BK47
4:29		BK38, BK63
5:1–2		BK85
5:14–20		BK34
6:10–18		BK45
6:10–20		BK73
	Exodus	
20:1–17		BK31
20:3		BK62, BK66
20:4–6		BK17
	Ezekiel	
12		BK88
	Galatians	
3:24		BK31, BK32
5:22–23		BK85
6:9		BK07
	Hebrews	
1:12		BK11
10:17		BK01, BK21
12:1		BK23
12:2		BK05, BK26
13:5		BK24, BK51, BK75
13:8		BK11, BK75
	Isaiah	
53:1–5		BK25
55:8		BK106
58:8–12		BK98
64:4		BK105
	James	
1:17		BK11, BK105, BK106
4:6		BK106
4:8		BK24
4:14		BK05
	Jeremiah	
29:11		BK52, BK92

21:9		BK40
26:17		BK40

Psalms

16:11	BK107
19:12	BK97
21:11–13	BK45
22:16	BK25
51:10	BK97
103:12	BK01
118:24	BK47, BK107
119:100–105	BK63
119:105	BK41
139:14	BK91
142:1–2	BK78

Revelation

1:14–17	BK102
2:12:17	BK50
3:14–20	BK77
19:11–16	BK100
21:1–5	BK57
21:1–4	BK80

Romans

1:20	BK91
2:6–10	BK07
3:23	BK10
5:8	BK52, BK59
8:18	BK42
8:26	BK06, BK08, BK29
8:26	BK38
8:28	BK62
8:34	BK78
12:2	BK21, BK22
12:1–2	BK21
12:3–8	BK04

INDEX

A

B

C

G

H

Maravich, Press	BK31, BK50, BK63, BK68, BK75
McAulay, Terry	BK65
McQueen, Dr. Michael	BK35
Mears, Henrietta	BK17
mercy	BK11, BK13, BK27, BK37, BK55, BK59, BK86, BK89, BK107
miracle	BK11, BK13
mission	BK16
Monroe, Earl	BK37
Moore, Maya	BK70

N

Nantz, Jim	BK101
Nash, Steve	BK71
Neal, Bert	BK57
Nichols, Henry (Hank)	BK65, BK97

O

obedience	BK27, BK47, BK53, BK79
Oldham, John	BK07
O'Neal, Shaquille	BK105

P

passion	BK26, BK45
perseverance	BK13, BK53, BK69, BK79, BK106, BK107
prejudice, taking a stand against	BK70
prophets, heed the warnings of the	BK87
Pullen, Jacob	BK83

Y

REFERENCES

BK01   *Marvin Webster*, http://en.wikipedia.org/wiki/Marvin_Webster

BK05   *Maravich*, Wayne Federman and Marshall Terrill in collaboration with Jackie Maravich-McLachlan, pp. 356–358

BK09   *Three-peat*, http://en.wikipedia.org/wiki/Three-peat

BK17   *Maravich*, Wayne Federman and Marshall Terrill in collaboration with Jackie Maravich-McLachlan, pp. 76–77

BK21   *Pete Maravich Testimony*, Jimmy Walker video, Phoenix, AZ, October 9, 1985

BK22   *Maravich*, Wayne Federman and Marshall Terrill in collaboration with Jackie Maravich-McLachlan, p. 326, pp. 328–329, p. 342, p. 350

BK27   *Maravich*, Wayne Federman and Marshall Terrill in collaboration with Jackie Maravich-McLachlan, p. 25

BK28   *Maravich*, Wayne Federman and Marshall Terrill in collaboration with Jackie Maravich-McLachlan, p. 323

BK31   *The Pistol*, Mark Kriegel, p. 132

BK35   *Amazing*, Pete Maravich video by Wayne Federman, *Amazing* by Aerosmith, 1989

BK35   *Mornings and Evenings with Spurgeon,* Charles H. Spurgeon, 1989

BK37   *Wall Must Complete Community Service,* http://espn. go.com, May 29, 2009

BK37   Mark Hall, "Slow Fade," http://castingcrowns.com, 2007

BK42   *Leader of the Pack,* http://sharingthevictory.com, 2007

BK43   *Beyond the Brass Ring,* http://powertochangeie/changed/pmaravich.html

BK44   *Eads Home Ministries, http://www.eadshomcom/David Robinson.htm,* July 17, 2006

BK46   Copy of a handwritten note owned by Dan Farr, entitled "From the desk of…Pete Maravich"

BK47   *Calipari Not Looking Ahead to Louisville Yet,* http://vaughtsviews.com/?p=2378 Larry Vaught, December 28, 2009

BK48   *Pete Maravich Testimony,* Shreveport, Louisiana 1986

BK50   *Maravich,* Wayne Federman and Marshall Terrill in collaboration with Jackie Maravich- McLachlan, p. 377

BK53   *My Utmost for His Highest,* Oswald Chambers, 1992, February 15

BK58   *Miracle,* Movie, 2004, directed by Gavin O'Connor, written by Eric Guggenheim

BK58   InTouch Ministries, http://www.intouch.org/resources/sermon-outlines/content/topic/our_god_of_grace_sermon_outline, Dr. Charles Stanley

BK58   *Coach Wooden One-on-One,* p. 137, Jay Carty and John Wooden

BK59   *Muhlenberg County Information Source,* Article by: Mike Fields, Lexington Herald-Leader

BK63   *Coach Wooden: One on One,* Day 55, Jay Carty and John Wooden

BK63   *How to Be Like Coach Wooden: Life Lessons from Basketball's Greatest Leader,* pp. 11–12, 2006, written by Pat Williams, David Wimbish, Bill Walton

BK66   *Maravich,* Wayne Federman and Marshall Terrill in collaboration with Jackie Maravich-McLachlan, p.122–124

BK67   *McDonald's "The Showdown"* (1993): Michael Jordan and Larry Bird, http://www.youtube.com/watch?v=oACRt-Qp-s

BK68   *Maravich,* Wayne Federman and Marshall Terrill in collaboration with Jackie Maravich-McLachlan, p.105

BK73   *The Pistol,* p.66, Mark Kriegel, 2008

BK77   *I Remember Pete Maravich,* pp. 67–68, Mike Towle, 2003

BK78   http://kentuckysportsradio.com, January 30, 2010

BK83   *5'10" White Kid Wins NCAA Slam Dunk Contest,* http://www.yardbarker.com/all_sports/articles/510_white_kid_wins_ncaa_slam_dunk_contest/4482838, April 3, 2011

BK84   *Josh "Jorts" Harrellson Is Relishing Every Moment Of Playing Time This March As The Wildcats Dance Into The Final Four,* http://sportsradiointerviews.com/2011/03/29/josh-jorts-harrellson-kentucky-wildcats-final-four, March 29, 2011, Steven Cuce

BK85   *Be Imitators of God,* This Day with the Master, Dr. Dennis Kinlaw, 2002

BK89   *Coach Wooden: One-on-One,* p. 118, Jay Carty and John Wooden, 2003

BK94   *Thunder's Kevin Durant commits to daily Bible reading,* http://newsok.com/thunders-kevin-durant-commits-to-daily-bible-reading/article/3560862, Darnell Mayberry, April 18, 2011

BK102   *I Can Only Imagine*, MercyMe, 2001

BK102   *One Shining Moment*, David Barrett Hodges, 1986

BK104   *Jeremy Lin's InterVarsity Roots*, http://www.intervarsity. org/news/jeremy-lins-intervarsity-root, Gordon Govier, February 14, 2012

BK107   *One Day at a Time*, Cristy Lane, 1974

CPSIA information can be obtained
at www.ICGtesting.com
Printed in the USA
LVOW04s0526040916

502952LV00003B/4/P